LIMITS OF UNBELIEF

JOHN KNOX

Limits of Unbelief

COLLINS
14 St James's Place, London
1970

SBN 00 215459 5

copyright © 1970 by John Knox

Printed in Great Britain by
Collins Clear-Type Press
London & Glasgow

Dedicated to
My Students and Colleagues
at the
Episcopal Theological Seminary of the Southwest
(1965–1970)
With Gratitude, Loyalty, and Affection

CONTENTS

Preface   9

1 THE PROBLEM OF BELIEF   11

2 BEGINNING WHERE WE ARE   28

3 CRITERIA OF TRUE BELIEFS   41

4 THE CHURCH AND CHRIST (I)   53

5 THE CHURCH AND CHRIST (II)   67

6 THE FATHER OF OUR LORD JESUS CHRIST   81

7 THE LIFE EVERLASTING   97

8 THE LAW OF CHRIST   108

   Index   121

PREFACE

I HAVE dedicated this small book to my students and colleagues in this Seminary in recognition of the warm welcome they gave me when I came here in 1965, for a single semester, and in 1966 for however many years of teaching might still be left me. But the more potent reason for the dedication, particularly as regards my students, lies in the fact that the book has been written, from beginning to end, with them and their wives especially in my mind. In conversations with them, many of whom have honoured and blessed me with their confidence, I have come to feel more poignantly than before both the rich spiritual reality of our fellowship in Christ and the urgent need for greater clarity and firmness in our beliefs about it. It is because I know that many others, experiencing this same reality, must also feel this need that I am venturing to share these essays with a wider circle of readers.

Two notes of a bibliographical kind are called for. The first chapter of this book was given, in substantially the same form, as the Page Lecture at the Berkeley Divinity School in New Haven, Conn., in April of 1968; and I am grateful to Dean Richard Wilmer and his colleagues for permission to use it here, as well as for the honour of being invited to give the Lecture and for many courtesies. I must also explain that several paragraphs in the seventh chapter were taken with some emendation from the Ingersoll Lecture on Immortality which I had the privilege of giving at Harvard University in 1960. Because that Lecture, revised and enlarged, was subsequently published as a small book by the Abingdon Press under the title *Christ and the Hope of Glory*, there are recognizable correspondences between a few paragraphs in the book and a few in the present work. I thank the Abingdon Press for allowing such repetition as there is and refer the reader of chapter seven to the earlier publication for a somewhat fuller discussion of the Christian hope than is possible in this book.

Episcopal Theological Seminary   JOHN KNOX
of the Southwest
Advent, 1968

Chapter 1

THE PROBLEM OF BELIEF

I T may seem much too obvious to need saying that the Christian Church is experiencing a crisis of belief—a crisis both unprecedented and of extraordinary scope and depth—but I can see no way of opening this discussion without saying it. Never have the traditional affirmations of faith been so vigorously challenged within the Church itself as just now. Never has the answer of Christians to the question, 'What do we believe?' been so hesitant and uncertain. And, on the more positive side, never has the work of theological reconstruction been so widely and so seriously undertaken, and at so radical a level. It would be gratuitous to offer evidence for such statements as these; nor, for my purpose, do I need to attempt any analysis of the cultural reasons for the developing crisis. The fact of it is inescapable; and nothing is clearer than that the Church stands in particular and urgent need of clarifying its intellectual position, of stating it in terms that are understandable and relevant, at the same time being faithful to its own distinctive life and history.

To this work of clarification I have no hope of making more than the minutest contribution, and I count on the reader's accepting and understanding the limits of my purpose. I am not rash enough even to think of attempting a definitive statement of the Church's faith, of proposing precisely formulated answers to the question, 'What are the essential beliefs of the Church?' or, 'What must (or does) the Christian believe?'—in a word, of presuming to define with any fullness or exactness the content of Christian 'orthodoxy'. On the other hand, I do want to share some convictions about the significance of these questions of belief, and about the perspective in which they should be considered, and to offer some hints at least of how answers may fruitfully be sought.

In the present chapter, however, we shall be occupied with a prior question, namely, 'Is it appropriate to speak of *any* belief as essential? Is believing in any particular way a necessary part of, or element in, Christian existence?' It is obvious that this question is logically prior, since there is no point in asking what the Church believes if one has concluded that it does not belong to the nature of the Church to believe anything. But it is almost equally clear that the question has more than a logical claim to be considered first; it is in actual fact, whether recognized as such or not, the basic, decisive question in the current discussion.

*   *   *

Before considering even this question, however, I need to state a presupposition or assumption. It needs to be stated because it lies as a conviction behind anything I may say on our theme, and it must be called a presupposition because it is not a demonstrable or even debatable proposition, but is, if allowed at all, something 'given' in the Christian man's experience. I have in mind nothing other than the reality of the Church—its actual existence, in the rich, more-than-merely-factual, sense that term has acquired. I shall assume that we agree—and agree, not merely hypothetically as a prelude to argument, but really agree on the ground of our experience—that the Church, to which we belong, is a real, identifiable community in human history, unique as all concrete things are, a living body whose life is inseparably its own, an organic cultural reality of consistent and distinctive quality and of great inner richness and power. This body exists, as it has existed since the first century. Its vitality, as well as its influence, may wax or wane. But it is still, as it has always been, characteristically and recognizably itself; and those who share most deeply in its life will know both its integrity and its distinctive identity.

In the present period of revolutionary social change, in which all our established institutions and their ways are involved, the Church has been challenged, as rarely if ever before, to demonstrate its relevance—more than that, to *be*, or to *become*, relevant. No one will deny that this challenge is needed. Nothing is clearer than that the Church must be radically reformed if it is truly and fully to serve the present age; but it is also just as clear that it must be radically reformed if it is fully and truly to realize its own nature. The maintaining, or regaining, of the Church's relevance is also a maintaining, or regaining, of its own authentic being as the particular community it is; it can be distinctively useful only as it is distinctively itself. The reformed or renewed Church will still be the Church, continuous with the ancient events in which it had its birth and bearing the marks of this historical connection. We are being told by many of our prophets that the Church must lose itself in service to its age. This is surely true; but the 'losing' which is, or should be, meant is that kind of 'losing' which is also a 'finding'—the Church finding itself in a renewed realization of its singular and historically given vitality.

So, at least, the Christian man, in virtue of his existence as such, will think of it. It will be impossible for him to think of the Church as losing itself in the sense of being simply inundated by, absorbed into, the secular order. He is too deeply and poignantly aware of its peculiar reality and of his own intimate and total involvement in it to consider such a possibility. The detached observer may reach other conclusions as regards both the value and the destiny of the community; but the Christian man is, by definition, not a detached observer. He cannot be such; nor indeed, in a case like this, can anyone *really* be. For to be 'detached' one would have to lose sight of, or perhaps never to have seen, what one is presumably 'observing'. This is a consideration which will be more pertinent perhaps at a later point in this discussion. At the moment the point is only that we are assuming the existence of the Church and that I am seeking to speak for persons who belong to that existence and are deeply concerned in it and about it.

*   *   *

This being understood, we turn to the question proposed a moment ago; and at once I find what I want to say more difficult to state and know that many a reader will find it more questionable. What I should want to say is something like this: The Christian existence of which I have been speaking involves an element of intellectual belief. It implies the acceptance as true of certain facts and ideas, the assent of the *mind* to them— facts and ideas which may, or may not, be generally accepted or be generally acceptable. The acknowledgment of this essential character of Christianity is dangerous because it may so easily lead into what, from any intelligent and free-minded person's point of view, will seem a rigid and intolerant dogmatism or an obscurantist fundamentalism. How the acknowledgment can be made, and made firmly and clearly, without such consequences—as I believe it can be—will appear, I hope, as this discussion proceeds. But, whatever the consequences, I do not see how one can avoid the acknowledgment itself. Being a Christian means, among other things, believing something—or, better said perhaps, *seeing* with one's *mind, thinking* about, the world and human life in certain characteristic ways.

I have hinted at the inability of many, even many Christians, readily and clearly to recognize this fact; and it may be appropriate to refer to two of the more important grounds of the difficulty—the more so because the difficulty is one all Christians are bound in some measure to feel.

The first of these grounds is the fact, already implied, that Christianity is not an ideology, in the way Marxism, for example, may be said to be. In the concrete wholeness of the Christian's life, memory and feeling seem to have a more basic place than thinking. The Christian shares in certain communal remembrances and in a certain communal spirit—and this, he may conclude, is the whole of what he shares in. Common *thoughts* are not to be expected. One may *remember* and *feel* with others, being caught up in a common experiencing of reality, past and present, a common sensing of its quality; but one must *think* alone. Thus, we Americans may remember and feel as Americans, but we think simply as the individuals we are—at any rate, we know that this is the only proper and honest way to think, that unless we are thinking individually and independently we are not truly *thinking*, not to say thinking *truly*. How, then, can it be otherwise with us as Christians, or indeed as members of any organic community? How can intellectual opinions be anything other than basically irrelevant? Even more to the point: How can any particular opinion or opinions be acknowledged as belonging essentially to such an existence?

The second ground of our difficulty in making this acknowledgment lies in the nature of the language which the Church characteristically uses, and indeed must use, in expressing the reality of its existence. This language is more than ordinarily allusive in character, emotionally connotative, richly metaphorical, full of inherited symbolic terms whose continuing *usefulness* consists in our finding in them the same concrete meanings which they originally expressed but whose continuing *usability* depends upon our understanding their relation to factual or ontological truth in a radically different way—more particularly, the language of the Church is to a considerable degree mythological language. This being true, one has, and cannot escape having, whether one recognizes it or not, a wide freedom in *interpreting* the language. But since one knows that the language does not mean just what it says, can one say that it certainly means anything at all? To be sure, one will recognize that it expresses something of the concrete, felt character of the Church's life, and that therefore it is immensely valuable, even indispensable; only in such language, essentially the language of art, can the *quality* of Christian experience, or of any experience, be caught up and communicated. But that true *facts* and true *ideas* need to be found in this language, or can be—that is quite another matter.

The issue clearly arises in connection with the Creeds. 'I believe', says the Christian worshipper, beginning to say the Apostles' or the Nicene Creed—but does he? He will go on to say some things which, almost certainly, he does not believe, if 'believe' is understood in the ordinary sense of accepting some statement as factually accurate. Is it not clear, then, that the word is not being used in that sense and that in saying, 'I believe', the Christian is saying only: 'I find myself at home within the historic Christian community; I share, and want to share, in its life, of which this ancient formulation is a symbol'? Imagine (the argument will continue) a creed written in philosophical or scientific terms, a creed that could be 'believed' (or not) in the ordinary sense, a creed that conveyed clear conceptions—is a creed of this kind a possibility, or even conceivable? Imagine, if you can, a creed which, instead of beginning simply with 'I believe in God', undertook also to state an *idea* of God. In such a case, whose idea of God would it

be? Would it be Tillich's or Whitehead's? Would it be
Berkeley's or Leibnitz' or Spinoza's? Would it be Anselm's or
Aquinas' or William of Ockham's? Would it be Augustine's
or Plotinus'? Since it is obvious that it might conceivably be
any of these, and many more, and that any of them may be
true, or more true than others, and that none of them, and no
combination of them, needs to be—since this is obvious, must
we not say that the statement, 'I believe in God', is without
definite intellectual content? It is the expression of an emotional
and moral attitude or disposition toward reality, not of an
intellectual understanding of it. And—the plausible argument
may conclude—the same thing can be said of all religious, and
particularly of all Christian, language. In other words, there
could not be a necessary Christian belief, because there is no
way in which such a belief could be definitively stated.

So much by way of a summary statement of two objections,
closely related if not basically identical, to any attempt to
identify an element of necessary belief in Christian existence.
What shall one say in reply to them?

*　　*　　*

One must begin, I think, by recognizing their truth and
weight. It is indubitably true that Christianity is essentially an
existence, not a philosophy or theology, and that its characteristic language is appropriate to its nature. Terms like 'the love
of God', his 'grace' and 'truth', 'reconciliation', 'new life in
Christ', 'joy', 'peace', and 'hope' in 'the Spirit'—these are not
philosophical, or even in the first instance theological terms,
but are terms answering to, expressive of, the rich concrete
reality of the Church's life. In so far as the Christian can be
identified by his language, it will not be by his being able
verbally, and however literally, to subscribe to some formulation of Christian *belief*, ancient or modern; but, rather, by his

ability to use with naturalness and sincerity and a profound sense of reality the devotional language of the Church. Or perhaps it would be more accurate to find the identifying mark—again, so far as one's language can provide it—not so much in one's ability to *use* this language as in one's inability to *avoid* using it. For the terms in which this language consists are inseparable from authentic Christian existence and stand in a necessary reciprocal relation to the Christian life itself—the life informing and giving meaning to the terms, and the terms informing and giving meaning to the life. The words and phrases are almost as concrete as the experienced reality out of which they arise and to which they refer. And they constitute the indispensable, and I believe we must say, the only indispensable, language of the Church. The recognition of this fact is expressed in the emphasis often laid upon the ability to participate sincerely in the Church's worship as the adequate, and only adequate, test of one's being an authentic sharer in the Church's faith.

But all of this being granted, we cannot conclude that the whole question of intellectual belief is irrelevant. This is true for at least two reasons, which I shall now briefly discuss.

The first is that philosophical or scientific language is not the only language in which beliefs, even true beliefs, can be expressed. One can obviously go beyond this negative statement and point out that there are innumerable honest and intelligent beliefs—that is, opinions or judgments which we understandably, even necessarily, regard as true—which cannot be expressed in this language. It would obviously be arbitrary to say *a priori* that such beliefs cannot be trusted or that we have no right to them. I can be as certain of the loyalty of a person whom I intimately know as I can be of a logical conclusion from the most self-evident of premises. I can as surely believe, and believe as surely, that a remembered experience of my own really occurred as that a straight line is the shortest distance between two points. (As a matter of fact, in view of current developments in science, may it not be that, in the particular instance, I can be more sure of the former?) If 'believing' means 'knowing absolutely', it is arguable that the word is inappropriately applied to *any* of our opinions in *any* realm of our life and thought; and in that case we can be said truly to 'believe' nothing at all. But the word does not need to be defined in so fantastic a way. If it were, we should have to find another term to denote the felt certainty we *can* have of truth; and my point just now is that this 'felt certainty' often pertains to a kind of 'truth' which cannot be neatly—that is, precisely and exhaustively—expressed in philosophical or scientific terms, or indeed in definitive terms of any kind.

This is true, not only because of the concrete nature of experienced reality, but also because of our own nature as men. Our existence is that of persons who have minds as well as sensibilities, affections and wills; or, to say the same thing more accurately, as persons we respond *intellectually* to what is disclosed in experience, as well as physiologically, aesthetically, emotionally, morally, and in other ways. It belongs to the very nature of our human life that wherever there is experience there is also the effort to understand it; indeed, so close is the relationship that some intellectual reflection is an ingredient of the experience itself. Our existence is realized as having a structure, the discerning and affirming of which are felt to be a discerning and affirming of truth. Such truth may not be demonstrable and may not be susceptible of statement in the publicly understood terms of intellectual discourse, but, given the reality of the existence, it may still be true—I mean, not merely true for the experiencing person, but really, objectively, true.

Now Christianity, as we have seen, is primarily an existence, something actual, organic, contingent, historical, cultural, concrete. Because it is this kind of thing, and not a system of ideas, or even an aggregation of people who share the same ideas—on this account a certain kind of propositional creed, in terms belonging to universal intellectual discourse, is inappropriate and impossible. But, for the same reason, another kind of creed is not only appropriate and possible, but is essentially present, whether recognized and confessed or not. This is the creed which consists in the ascribing of reality to the distinctive existence of the Church in all its inner richness and in the acknowledging of the truth of what, from the point of view of the participant in it (who alone can know what it is), is manifestly implied in that existence. The point is, not that there should be such a creed, or that there may be, but that there *is*: an element of belief is inescapably involved in Christian life itself.

This involvement of belief in life may be exemplified by a reference to the Church's worship, where, it will be at once agreed, the Christian's life as a Christian is more directly and immediately expressed than in any conceivable statement of what he believes about anything. Only a moment ago I referred to the point frequently made that the only proper criterion of one's sharing in the Church's faith is one's ability to participate sincerely in the Church's worship. If one has to say one thing or the other, it is undoubtedly more nearly true to say that we believe because we pray than to say that we pray because we believe. But even if we should find the statement, 'We believe because we pray', *entirely* true and adequate, it would still need to be recognized that we do in fact *believe*. We may have exposed the psychological ground of our believing, but we have not ceased doing it. We may have *explained* our believing, but we have not explained it *away*. Our statement, 'We believe', still stands. In the *lex orandi, lex credendi* the *credendi* is as important as the *orandi*, whatever the proper order is taken to be.

For in our 'praying' we experience, and existentially respond to, reality in a way of which, in our 'believing', we seek to give some rational account. We cannot help seeking to do this since we are rational persons; and just as surely and for the same reason, we cannot forever tolerate a discrepancy between our rational conclusions about life and the world, on the one hand, and the necessary rational presuppositions of our devotional acts, on the other. It may be true that we believe because we pray; but it is also true that we may cease to pray—that is, to pray consciously, intentionally, habitually, effectually—because we shall have ceased to believe. A recent Report of an Episcopal Church commission in the United States[1] cites as a criterion of orthodoxy the ability 'sincerely and responsibly to join . . . in the celebration of God's being and goodness in the prayers and worship of the Prayer Book'. I am in complete sympathy with what is said in the paragraphs where this point is being made, but only if I give the weight I am sure the commission itself gave to the phrases 'sincerely and responsibly' and, later, 'with a consenting mind'. For, in the long run, for the Prayer Book language, or any devotional language, to be *used*, its basic doctrinal presuppositions and assertions must be *believed*. This fact points up the necessity of liturgical reform; but it also reminds us that certain intellectual beliefs do belong essentially to the Christian existence.

The gap between liturgy and theology, between worship and belief, which, I sometimes think, is particularly noticeable in the Episcopal Church (my own Church)—perhaps in Anglican churches generally—must certainly engage the attention of the

[1] Stephen Bayne, ed., *Theological Freedom and Social Responsibility: Report of the Advisory Committee of the Episcopal Church* (New York: Seabury Press, 1967).

theological commission which the Report envisages. Such a commission, indeed, might conceivably start with the Prayer Book and ask two questions: 1) What changes from the point of view of concern for theological truth do we believe need to be made in the language of this book? and 2) In the Book as thus revised what in the way of theological truth is clearly and unmistakably implied?

*   *   *

This last query may serve to introduce the second element in the reply I would make to the argument that, owing to the nature of the Church and consequently of its language, the whole question of normative Christian belief is not only unanswerable but also irrelevant. This second point is the suggestion that although it may indeed be impossible to express in a precise or definitive form the positive content of Christian belief, it *may* be possible for us, proceeding in more negative fashion, to indicate limits beyond which it cannot go without denying and betraying the existence to which the Christian belongs. It may be true that no belief, stated at all precisely, can be *included* as necessary; but may it not be that some beliefs can be *excluded* as impossible?

Acknowledging that this is true would not mean conceding that Christian belief may not have, and does not have, a positive content. After all, to define is to set limits; and it often happens in a given case that if the limits are to be set at all precisely, it can be only with reference to what lies beyond them. When my family owned a farm in New England, we could indicate its general area with a wave of the hand; but when we sold the property and had to identify it exactly, the deed could do so only by naming the owners of the contiguous lands. Similarly, we customarily define the area of a country by indicating what lies beyond its borders. So also there are many

situations in ordinary life in which we can be surer and clearer
about what is wrong than about what is right, about what is
false than about what is true. We often find ourselves saying,
'*That* I cannot *do*', meaning, 'Though I am uncertain as to what
I may properly do in this situation, the thing proposed is
definitely out of bounds; I must not and will not do it.' Or we
may say, '*That* I cannot believe.' Our beliefs about the integrity
of another person, for example, are often thus expressed, and
perhaps could be expressed with any precision only thus. We
say, 'I cannot believe he would act in the way you have
described,' or 'I know he would not have said what has been
reported.' Such rejections of alleged truth obviously represent
a way of indicating what we believe to be the real truth. And
when we ask, 'What does the Christian believe?', we cannot
escape the necessity of making such negations. Thus, the
identification of the 'heretical' may be, not only a way, but
even the indispensable way, to the identification of orthodoxy.

Years ago I tried to write something on the normative value
of the early Church, its significance for what Theodore O.
Wedel has taught us to speak of as 'the coming great Church'.[2]
I sought to give full recognition to the wide diversity of early
Christianity, but without losing sight of its basic unity and
identity. In emphasizing this latter, I had no trouble, as it
seemed to me, in identifying, and describing in positive terms,
what I called the 'shared life'—the inner reality, the felt
quality, of the primitive Christian existence as expressed, for
example, in Paul's letters, or in I Peter, or in the Johannine
gospel and epistles. But having done this as well as I was able,
I realized that something needed also to be said about a
'common faith'. For, manifestly, the early Christians did more
than share in a common experience; they also did some

[2] In a book with this title published in New York by Macmillan Company
in 1945 and in London by SCM in 1947.

'believing' together. But when I tried to identify this element in the common existence, I found, without my intending it so or even being aware at the time of its being so, that my speech fell into negative terms. I found myself defining, not beliefs the early Christian would necessarily have held, but rather beliefs he would necessarily have rejected. How I identified these off-limits beliefs is not to the point just now. I am concerned only with the principle and the method, and with the fact that when it came to saying in any precise way what the primitive Christians agreed in believing, I simply found myself saying what they agreed, or would have agreed, in denying. All I could do, I discovered when it came to speaking of the early Church's essential beliefs, was to say that there were certain beliefs 'which its very existence as the Church would always have kept it from embracing, no matter how subtle the temptation or how potent the pressure.'

Is this not true of the Church in every age? It is a very familiar fact that the ancient Creeds, although for the greater part couched in positive terms, are really concerned rather with ruling out false beliefs than with stating true ones. Is not a necessary logic, as well as an historical appropriateness, to be seen in this fact? The Church cannot say precisely what it believes—it has not the language for that kind of discourse. Besides, it would violate its nature as the organic historical (as distinguished from ideological) community it is if it should even try to set up any statement of this kind as a criterion of membership in Christ. But the fact that it cannot in this precise way state essential or normative beliefs does not mean that it is not able to judge between beliefs, on the one hand, which may or may not be true but can be tolerated and, on the other, beliefs which are clearly both false and destructive.

This can be said because the very sharpness which is characteristic of intellectual beliefs of a propositional kind and which accounts for the Church's difficulty in stating its own—this very sharpness makes possible its recognizing those beliefs which clearly are not, and cannot be, its own, because they are in effect denials of its existence. In the essay Professor J. V. L. Casserley contributed to the Report already referred to, he makes a very telling point when he writes: 'Heresy is much less tolerant than orthodoxy . . . The heretic is the man who knows the precise truth . . . He . . . really knows, and what he knows is precisely that orthodoxy is not simple enough. For him all truth is simple . . . The orthodox formulas, on the other hand, since they are primarily ways of negating heresy are much less specific as to what truth is.' We have seen that there are other reasons also—less utilitarian, more intrinsic and basic— for this lack of specificity. And is not Professor Casserley right in emphasizing the breadth, the flexibility—is it not correct to say with him, the catholicity?—of orthodoxy as compared with heresy? Orthodoxy in our time permits many beliefs about God and says finally we cannot know or say fully and definitively *what* God is; heresy either says in some simple or unitary way what he is or, even more simply, denies that he is at all. Orthodoxy permits many beliefs about how it was that in Christ God acted for us men and for our salvation and knows that no possible explanation of Christ will be adequate. Heresy either denies forthwith that such a divine action in history did, or could take place, or makes the same denial in less direct ways by describing the Church in purely sociological terms and by seeing it as fully contained and explained within what are understood to be the naturalistic continuities of history. Orthodoxy is full of the hope of the life everlasting but is unable to express the content of it in any definitive way; heresy simply denies that there is any such thing.

We must recognize, I think, that orthodoxy has not always been true to its nature in this respect (and here, perhaps, I would find myself drawing somewhat away from Professor Casserley—though, I hope, not too far). Orthodoxy has often been in the position of setting against the simple rigid belief of the heretic an equally simple and rigid belief of its own. In such a case it is arguable that both beliefs are heretical in the sense of being divisive and destructive; and also, paradoxically enough, that a true orthodoxy would have included both—included both, not by insisting on the truth of *both* of two mutually exclusive beliefs (*this* it often did), but rather, by allowing *either*. For this reason I do not think that all the ancient 'heresies' were, from a true, and therefore liberal or catholic, orthodoxy's point of view, real heresies (although some of them undoubtedly were); much less do I think that all modern opinions having some similarity or correspondence with opinions rejected by the Fathers are *ipso facto* to be rejected (although, again, some of them certainly must be). We can be instructed by the Fathers, and need to be; but the terms Arianism, Nestorianism, and the like, no longer apply. We must identify the heretical in terms of current ideas in their current context, and must decide, on the basis of our experience as participants in the historical Church, of our own integrity, and of our best judgment, what ideas tend to be destructive of, because they are in fact denials of, the existence of the Church.

Are such ideas being held and expressed? Surely we must agree that they are. Should we try to identify and define them? If we have answered 'Yes' to the first question, we can hardly fail to make an affirmative answer also to this one. Can we succeed? Here our reply is bound to be more doubtful. To be sure, individuals will reach assured conclusions; but can the Church do so? Can the Church succeed in identifying and defining those opinions in our own time which necessarily imply a denial of validity to the memory, faith, hope, love, thankfulness and praise, which are its life? This identification and definition will be hard to achieve; but, within broad limits, I should say it is not impossible. The term 'within broad limits' must not be thought of as representing a concession. For the 'limits' must be broad if they are to be true. The new orthodoxy will need to be liberal and catholic, not only to be feasible, but to be orthodox. The achieving of this new, liberal, and catholic orthodoxy, contemporary but at every truly essential point faithfully Christian, is not the least important of the many demanding tasks the Church faces in our time. It should be recognized as a task both necessary and possible, in the doing of which each of us can have a part.

Chapter 2

BEGINNING WHERE WE ARE

WE have seen, not only that the Christian has a right to say, 'I believe', but also that in virtue of his nature as a man and his being as a Christian, he is bound to speak so: in other words, that a creed of some kind, a statement of belief, is implicit in the Christian existence. This 'creed', we have also seen, will be basically a confession of what is actually found in this existence (which itself is a concrete, organic, historical thing); and therefore it will not consist either in affirmations of alleged scientifically demonstrable facts (whether of nature or history) or in abstract philosophical statements. Its language will consequently be less exact than the language of either science or philosophy. But although this must be said (and said not at all defensively) about the positive content of the 'creed', one must recognize that it may, and indeed inevitably will, imply a denial or rejection of any ideas or facts alleged to be true, whether stated in scientific or philosophical terms, which are themselves denials or rejections of what is given in the concrete existence to which the 'creed' belongs and of whose content it is a confession.

If this way of understanding what might be referred to as the place or status of belief in the life of the Church is anywhere near to being true, I venture to suggest that the responsibility of the Christian theologian in our time (or in any time) could be analysed, at least for purposes of discussion, into five parts: his task is (a) to realize as fully as possible the content of the Church's existence; (b) to observe as truly as possible what is the essential structure of this concrete reality or what are its essential elements; (c) to explicate the language, verbal and other, in which the Church expresses the meaning of its existence, translating it as fully and exactly as possible, into the terms of rational discourse, thus designating as sharply as possible the *truth* to be found in it; (d) to show the consonance of this truth with all that is known to be true in all the areas of human experience and, more than that, its power to illuminate that total experience and to enhance its significance; and (e) to identify as accurately as possible those beliefs and judgments, whether as regards facts or values, which the participant in the existence of the Church must as such know to be untrue.

To describe in such a way the theologian's task is to put the accomplishment of it beyond the grasp of any individual, however gifted or learned, and, in my own case, far beyond my 'reach' as well. But especially in view of the present confusion, no Christian theologian (and one might just as appropriately say, no Christian) can fail to feel an obligation to work at it, and to do, if not all that is 'possible', at least all that is possible *for him*. I shall make no effort to deal systematically with the five points in the proposed analysis, and the structure of our discussion will not be determined by them. I shall be concerned only to illustrate the relevance and value of this way of understanding the theological task by considering it as a whole in relation to several of the fields of theological concern —namely, the doctrines of the Church, of Christ, of God, of life after death, and of the Christian ethical norm. I shall, however, follow the order indicated in the analysis at least to the extent of devoting the present chapter to a consideration of the first two points proposed.

*   *   *

We begin, then, with the assertion that the Christian theologian's first responsibility is that of realizing the content of the Church's distinctive existence. By 'realizing' I mean acquiring or possessing the kind of experiential knowledge which derives from, if indeed it may not be said to consist in, a conscious sharing in that existence. It is possible that the possessing or acquiring of this knowledge should be thought of, not as a necessary element in the Christian theologian's *task*, but rather as a necessary precondition of his being a Christian theologian at all. But however this may be, and whether the state of being a Christian—that is, of really belonging to the Church, knowing it from within, sensing its distinctive quality, loving it for what it is deeply felt to be—whether being a Christian in this sense is to be regarded in the one way or the other, one must not fail to recognize its basic character and its absolute indispensability. In the preceding chapter it was urged that the existence of the Church was a necessary precondition of there being a normative Christian theology at all, whether as fact or possibility; now I am saying that the first responsibility—or, if you will, the first qualification—of one who would contribute to the determination of this theology must be actual participation in that same existence.

The reason I hesitate somewhat as to the terms here—whether to say 'responsibility' or 'qualification'—is that the 'participation' we are considering is, to a degree, subject to the will. If that were not true, the second term would obviously be the only appropriate one. I recall hearing a teacher of mine, an eminent theologian of a generation ago, say that he no longer went to church because, with the teaching and other work he had to do, he would not have been able to write his theological books if he had done so. I do not know what he did in order to stay in communion with the Church, in order to *be* in his personal life a sharer in its existence. Perhaps he found, and was nourished by, the reality of the Church in his intercourse with his students and colleagues; perhaps he knew this reality through participating in the life and work of a group devoted to prayer or to some kind of special service in Christ's name; or perhaps it was through meditation in communion with St Paul or St John or St Augustine or some other Christian, in the reading of whose written words the life of the Church can to a degree be felt and shared in. There may be many ways of 'going to church', and I do not know which of them my old teacher, or many another particular theologian, may have adopted. What I do know, or believe I know, is that unless one does in some way 'go to church'—that is, unless one is an actual participant in the shared life which is the Church—one cannot be an adequate interpreter of that life, whether as preacher or theologian.

Moreover—must one not also say?—it is precisely such an interpreter the Christian theologian, as truly as the Christian preacher, is called to be. His peculiar subject matter is obviously not the cosmos, or even human existence as such—this subject matter he shares with many others—but is the Church and *its* existence. And not only is this his *distinctive* subject matter; from first to last he is primarily concerned with it. This is the 'given', the *a priori*, the existential ground of his thought. He is moved primarily by a desire to see, and as fully as possible to understand, what is given as fact or possibility in this new creation in history, this new communal existence, of which his own existence is a part. This does not mean, I hope there is no need to say, that he will not be profoundly concerned with the cosmos and the totality of human existence; but his way of experiencing the cosmos and human existence as a whole will be determined in considerable part by his being as a Christian. He will find what seems to him to be the true clue to their meaning in the existence of the Church. Once the theologian loses his sense of the inner reality of this historical community and of his own identity within it, finds the concrete existential terms in which this reality has expressed itself from the beginning, no longer a living language, rich with meaning— once this happens, the theologian, no more than the preacher, has anything distinctively Christian to say. He may be able to contribute significantly, in tangential and often supportive ways, to the total theological enterprise, but he has surrendered his right, because he has lost his power, to be himself a creative partner in it. One cannot interpret what one does not know.

Lest this sound harsh, let me hasten to make clear that my only purpose is to affirm and emphasize a *principle*—namely, that the basic responsibility (or qualification) of the Christian theologian is to share in the Christian existence. I am not proposing any judgment upon particular theologians, past, present or future. As a matter of fact, once we turn our attention from the principle, we are involved in all kinds of uncertainties and relativities. The communal existence itself can be more, or less, authentic and is never, in any particular expression of it, a pure and perfect thing; and one's sharing in it can be more, or less, real and profound. It is probably safe to say that no Western theologian could fail to share in it at all, just as it is certainly true to say that none could share in it perfectly or completely. But, even so, the principle stands: The first thing a Christian theologian must be is a Christian; and the measure (if I may so speak) of his being a Christian— that is, the degree of fullness and authenticity in his participation in the existence of the Church—will set a limit in advance upon his ability to be a Christian theologian, no matter what his qualifications of learning, intelligence and imagination may be.

'Yes'—the objector may say—'and this same "measure" will set a limit upon his liberty as a thinker.' This claim that the Christian theologian, especially if thought of as being related to the Church in the complete and intimate way I have tried to describe, cannot be free is both plausible and prevalent and should be at least briefly examined. It assumes, I should say, that Christianity is primarily an ideology rather than being, as it is, a social existence. Basically, or in principle, there is no more validity, or sense, in saying that a Christian cannot be intellectually free than in saying a Frenchman or an Englishman cannot be intellectually free. Now it must be granted that the Englishman, or the Frenchman, is unable to believe to be true what as an Englishman or a Frenchman he knows not to be true, or to believe to be untrue what as an Englishman or a Frenchman he knows to be true. One cannot affirm as truth what is denied by one's existence or deny as truth what is revealed there. But if inability to deny such truth (or to affirm such untruth) is regarded as a lack of freedom, then it must be recognized that no one is free, or should be, and that intellectual freedom is a pure abstraction. And who would define freedom in any such way?

It may be objected that the Englishman or Frenchman does not, or at any rate should not, *think* as an Englishman or Frenchman, but simply as a man. One may fully and vigorously agree, and moreover go on to insist just as strongly that the Christian also does, or at any rate should, think as a man. Logic does not vary with nationality or religion, or the process of thinking with historical conditioning. If we think truly, we think humanly and we think together. But the *experience* or the existential knowledge with which our thinking is concerned *does* vary. To say that an Englishman must think, not as an Englishman, but as a man, is not to say that he may not *as an Englishman* know things to think about which men of other nationalities do not know. Is his thinking about these things necessarily less true or are the beliefs about them which he may arrive at necessarily less freely reached because this can be said?

I recognize that the analogy between belonging to the Church and belonging to a nation is not exact or perfect. Belonging to the Church involves us in a wider range and deeper level of concrete knowing than does our nationality, and consequently entails thinking and believing about matters of greater, indeed of ultimate, concern. But it is still true that the thinking and believing of the Christian can be as free as the thinking and believing of any man. The situation is not that he is a Christian because he has decided to think and believe in certain ways; rather, he finds himself thinking and believing in certain ways because he is a Christian. Only in these ways can he understand and interpret his existence as the man he is. If believing what one finds to be the truth is limiting, then one must concede that the Christian theologian is thus bound. But what is intellectual liberty itself except precisely that bondage?

*   *   *

From the beginning of this discussion I have spoken of the Church as a cultural organism in history, a living, growing community of a unique and recognizable kind, and have made no reference to the divergent, and often divisive, organizational structures which have characterized it. I have spoken of the Church as an 'existence', and to do this is to lay an emphasis upon its inner nature, its felt quality, as distinguished from any particular organizational form its life has taken or from all such forms together. This distinction is, from my point of view, of the greatest importance; and the recognition that whenever I speak of the Church in this book I am doing so in this 'existential' or 'qualitative' sense is indispensable to an understanding of its argument. A serious doubt may be felt, however, as to whether this distinction can validly be made, and before going further we must give some attention to this question.

Almost at once what was felt at first as a single question is seen in fact to be two: first, whether an actual, identifiable social reality, a distinctive recognizable community, can be discerned, can be truly said to exist, within and beneath the many changing and divergent forms of organization and practice to which I have referred; and, secondly (if that question is answered affirmatively), whether it is appropriate to refer to this reality, this community, as 'the Church'. These two questions are obviously separable and it is important that they be considered separately.

As for the first, I should think there could be very little difference of opinion among Christians. We do in fact find ourselves sharing in a common life with persons who belong to other 'churches' than our own. We are constantly and spontaneously recognizing our brethren in Christ across all the lines which in some respects separate us. I am not meaning to disparage the importance of some of these 'lines', and certainly I am not denying their reality. Indeed, in the present connection, it would not suit my purpose to do so even if I could. For the more certainly real and important these dividing lines are seen to be, the more certainly real and important must be the communal existence which, across them or beneath them, is actually found and experienced. I think of a Roman Catholic nun teaching in an eastern college with whom I have often shared my deepest concerns, of two Roman Catholic scholars with whom I have closely collaborated over an extended period, of several Eastern Orthodox graduate students and at least one priest whom I have known well, and of scores of other members of one or the other of these 'churches' with whom I have in some degree had the privilege of sharing my life and thought and who have lovingly shared theirs with me. I think of my own father, who did not belong to the 'church' of which I am now a member, and of hundreds of other Methodists through whom my spirit has been nourished, not to speak of a host of Protestants of all denominations. I think of a Quaker teacher in a theological seminary with whom at one time I lived and worked closely, and of many another Friend I have known and loved. I think in the same way of a Unitarian friend in the faculty of a northern university and of scores of so-called Pentecostals. I should find the statement that in my association with all of these I was not participating with them in an identifiable Christian social reality—I should find such a statement absolutely incredible, and I know that these persons would also find it so.

This truly catholic community, moreover, has existence not only among living persons, but in history as well. One finds oneself sharing with men and women of all the generations—with the ancient Fathers, and with Christian prophets, martyrs, saints, theologians, preachers, reformers in every century, in so far as these have left a witness to their life and thought. Above all, one finds oneself in communion with the earliest Christians—experiencing the same reality, participating in the same common life, that the writers of the New Testament knew. Paul, the authors of Ephesians and I Peter, John, and others of these writers, speak to us out of an existence we share with them. We are able to hear them because, in a sense, we already know what they have to tell us. They can speak *to* us because they also speak *for* us. For before they spoke at all, or perhaps were even *there* to speak, something had *happened*; and it is this happening, rather than anything they later said, which makes all the difference: a new social reality, a new kind of human association, a new *man*, had been brought into being. They could write as they did only because they belonged to this 'new creation', and we can understand what they wrote only because (and in the same degree) we also do. And yet not only did they not belong to any of our denominations, they antedated all of them. I repeat: Is it not transparently true, and do not all Christians agree, that there is a recognizable, distinctive social existence in history to which we belong (and in which we belong to one another), despite our differences and divisions, and at a deeper level?

It is when we ask the second question that the reply becomes more doubtful and discordant: Is it appropriate to refer to this social existence, this community of memory, of love, of hope as 'the Church'? Can this term properly be applied to the 'existential' or 'qualitative' reality we have been considering? Does not the word necessarily connote something definitive as regards form, as regards institutional structure and practice? This is obviously a much more debatable issue. Fortunately, however, for my purpose in this discussion it is not required that we reach a common answer. In two earlier books[1] I have attempted to state my own answer, and the reader who may be interested will learn there that I do not think any simple answer, either positive or negative, will suffice. He will discover that I do not regard the question of the form of the Church as indifferent, nor do I think we are without norms of it—norms which must be observed and followed (and not merely externally!) if there is ever to be in history a Church formally united. But, at the same time, it will be clear that I am not able to limit or circumscribe the Church by the application of any such formal tests. I am so deeply conscious of the community of mind and spirit under and across our divergences in form and am so strongly impressed by its supreme importance to the reality of the Church, however we define the word, that I cannot see any alternative to using that

[1] *The Early Church and the Coming Great Church* (Nashville and New York: Abingdon Press, 1955; London: Epworth Press, 1957); and *The Church and the Reality of Christ* (New York: Harper and Row, 1962; London: Wm. Collins Sons, 1963).

term in speaking of it. What other term would be adequate at all?

But this is only a question about words and, so far as the discussion of this book is concerned, is irrelevant so long as the reality and the paramount importance of the social existence we have been chiefly considering is acknowledged. If one does not want to call this existence the Church, one must find another term. The important thing is the recognition of the existence itself. It is of this existence I am speaking when I use the word 'Church' in this book.

*   *   *

The theologian's thinking about the Church will begin, I have said, with an effort at identification—an attempt 'to specify as truly as possible what is its essential structure and what are its essential elements.' I do not have in mind any effort to 'define' the Church. The Church is the Church, as England is England, and a rose is a rose. We can try to describe it, but the description of a concrete thing cannot be exhaustive or definitive. We can classify it according to some abstract scheme, but that is not to say what it is in its concrete uniqueness. What indeed can we do except to point to it, except to say, 'This is the Church'? And yet I believe there is at least one more thing we can do— although this, too, is a matter of 'pointing', not defining. Besides identifying the Church itself, we can identify elements in its concrete wholeness which seem to belong essentially to it—essentially in the sense that the reality of the Church as Church is unimaginable if these elements are not present.

This attempt at identification may seem to be a dubious undertaking because of the large subjective factor involved, and we shall not expect all Christians to agree with its results. But if we start, not with a preconceived idea of what the Church must be, not with the definition of a word, but with openness to, and a desire to recognize, the thing itself wherever we find it—then, I believe, there is a good chance of our agreeing, not only as to where and when the reality of the Church is found, but also as to some of the elements which in every instance belong to it—the elements, in fact, whose presence makes the Church recognizable and leads us to identify it as such.

Do I dare specify any such 'notes' of the Church? Having gone as far as I have, I cannot evade the obligation of trying to do so. I shall not seek to demonstrate the truth of the identifying marks I shall mention, nor will I attempt any exposition of what is meant concretely by each of them. Inferences to be drawn from them will engage us in subsequent chapters; but there is no point in attempting to prove their existence or to expose their concrete meaning. If the Christian reader should not find himself agreeing that the 'marks' are indeed invariable and essential, there would be no way of convincing him by arguments that they are such; and if he does not know already what they are in their concrete reality, no exposition could give him this knowledge. In such a case, one could only conclude that he and I experience the reality of the Church in different ways. Actually, however, I do not antici- pate any significant divergence—how could I, when what I think I am doing is simply pointing to constant and important features of a concrete reality which as Christians we all know? This does not mean, of course, that things other than I shall say could not also be truly said, or that what I shall say could not be said in other, and doubtless better, ways or put in a more appropriate order.

With these understandings, then, I venture to identify six elements in the existential reality of the Church: first, a sense of being the people of God—the God of Abraham, Isaac, and Jacob—and therefore of belonging to the same history as that to which Israel belonged and belongs; secondly, a reverent and loving memory of Jesus; thirdly, the experience of the Spirit apprehended as being both God's immanent reality as love and truth and the continuing presence of Jesus as Lord—experience evoking a characteristic response of adoration, thankfulness and love, and constituting a new and highly distinctive fellowship —a partnership in love of a quite unique kind; fourthly, the deeply felt conviction that in the event in which the Church arose a unique and redemptive self-revelation of God was taking place and that in the Church that event is in a real sense constantly recurring; fifthly, the confident expectation that God's true and loving purpose for his creation, 'the uniting of all things in Christ', will be fulfilled; and finally, the recognition that a distinctive way of feeling and acting towards all men (namely, the way of that same love) appertains essentially to this new existence and is therefore open to, and obligatory upon, those who share in it.

Can we imagine the Church without this sense of history, this memory, this experience, this conviction, this hope and this ethical awareness? Or can we imagine its finding acceptable any belief which denied what is essentially contained in them or necessarily implied by them? To a further examination of this question the rest of this book will be devoted.

Chapter 3

CRITERIA OF TRUE BELIEFS

THE principal aim of the preceding chapters has been to defend the thesis that the necessary presupposition of any Christian theology is the Church's existence and that the prime qualification of a Christian theologian is his own sharing in that existence. But always implied and frequently asserted has been the assumption that what the Church 'says' to us, by being what it is, is true; or, to speak more exactly, that when, as a Christian, one believes what one's life as a Christian necessarily implies, one is not only believing what by an inner necessity one must believe, but is also believing the truth. Such a judgment, I am saying, is the basic one in a distinctively Christian theology, and our purpose in this book is to consider what some of these necessary beliefs can be said to be.

Before turning more directly, however, to the consideration of this question, we need to say something at least about proper method in arriving at true beliefs.

*   *   *

We may appropriately begin with a reference to what is ordinarily called 'natural theology' and with some comment on the relation of this theology to the distinctively Christian theology which, I have been saying, always presupposes the Church's existence and the theologian's existence within it. I have no intention of discussing the relation between theology and philosophy in any broad or systematic way—a task for which I am obviously incompetent. But certain questions about this relation may well have been raised by what I have been saying; and it is perhaps not inappropriate that I try to indicate a general position. Am I setting the 'Christian theologian' over against the 'natural theologian', affirming a necessary antagonism or incompatibility and thus impugning the legitimacy of 'natural theology' from the Christian's point of view? Or is it only that I am questioning its relevance and fruitfulness? Neither of these things do I wish to do, or to seem to do. The one thing I want to do—the only thing which the thesis I am defending requires that I do—is to reject the notion that the two 'theologies' can be separated for the same theologian, and, more particularly, the notion that 'natural theology' is the first storey of an edifice of which 'Christian theology' is the second; or, to change the image, that 'natural theology' is the earlier stage of a journey of which 'Christian theology' is the later and consummating part.

This way of defining and ordering, for all its impressive authority and wide vogue, must be rejected because it does not take into account the concrete, existential basis of theology whether 'natural' or 'Christian'. It overlooks the fact that the Christian theologian is an actual person, formed by, and having his being in, a complex environment of nature and culture. He is not 'pure theologian'. Theology is not an abstraction. Theology is a theologian thinking. And the theologian must think as the total person he is. If he is a twentieth-century American Christian, any honest, serious thinking he does about God (or indeed about anything else of importance) will be the thinking of such a person. He may try to imagine how he would think if he were a twentieth-century Russian Christian, or a nineteenth-century American Christian, or a twentieth-century Chinese Buddhist; but he will not entirely succeed in such an undertaking, and in any case he will not be really thinking for himself. Nor can he separate between capacities or roles in himself, and think, now in one of them and now in another—now as an American, now as a modern man, now as a Christian. Again, he may play at doing this, but he cannot really succeed. It would be a self-conscious exercise of the mind; and genuine thinking is never self-conscious.

Moreover, the Church, in any given time or instance, is a complex and indivisible human reality. There is no such thing as 'pure Christianity' if by that phrase is meant some Christian 'essence', which can be distilled out of the concrete whole. Real Christianity—the only real Christianity—is the *Church*, the actual human community in history; and this Christianity involves as part of itself the whole culture of a given place and epoch. May we not say, then, that it is inappropriate, and in the last resort impossible, for the Christian theologian to begin his work by trying to imagine how he would think, and what he would believe, if he were not a Christian, and having laid this 'foundation', proceed to build on it a Christian superstructure? Whether he recognizes the fact or not, it will still be true that if he is thinking seriously and responsibly, he will be thinking as a Christian from beginning to end.

But it is just as manifest that, also from beginning to end, he will be thinking as the whole person he is. It is obvious that if he has developed the habit of logical thinking, his thinking as a theologian will tend to be logical. If his aesthetic perceptions are acute, his theological thought will be affected by this sensitivity. If through imagination or suffering he knows certain depths in human existence, his theological thought will bear the marks of this knowledge. If he is a competent historian, or scientist, or philosopher, he will not cease being such when he thinks theologically. If he has been influenced creatively by a particular scholar or school, he will not, as a Christian theologian, think and reach conclusions as though he had not been.

Not only will he not do so; he cannot do so. For he is the man he is; and if he is thinking seriously and reaching conclusions honestly, he must do so as *that man* in that man's concrete wholeness.

The dichotomy we are rejecting has, more often than not perhaps, been designated as a division between 'natural' and 'revealed' theology—the one comprising the truth we can arrive at for ourselves; the other, the truth divinely revealed to us. But this way of making the division is as false as the other. For there is no revealed *truth*, if by 'truth' is meant an *idea* or *fact* or a body of *ideas* or *facts*. All *truth* in this sense, at whatever level and of whatever kind, must be arrived at in the human and universal way—through critical reflection on experience. On the other hand, all *experience*, at whatever level and of whatever kind, is, or may be, revealing. Our knowledge of concrete *reality* (which, if we are to know it, must always 'reveal' itself to us) and our judgments about it (which, if they are to be true, must always be arrived at through the right exercise of our minds) are inseparable at every stage. So far as intellectual belief is concerned, the 'difference' of the Christian, as I have had occasion to say several times, consists, not in the fact that he thinks by a 'different' process from other men and (one may now add) not in the fact that, unlike other men, he is relieved or dispensed from thinking beyond a certain point, but rather in the fact that he has been given in his own experience as a person some 'different' things to think about. This is not to ascribe to the Christian some esoteric privilege. He knows a 'secret', to be sure, but the secret is an open one. The 'different things' are those belonging to the Church's existence, in which all men are lovingly called to share and are capable of sharing, fully and freely.

*   *   *

The assertion has just been made that although the Christian man's essential beliefs are in a sense 'given' him in and with his existence as a Christian, this fact does not mean that he is dispensed from the necessity of active and intelligent *thinking*. The necessity remains for the obvious reason that he stands in constant danger of seeing as *given*, facts and ideas which are *not* necessarily implied by the Christian existence and, therefore, are not really 'given' at all. The strictest honesty and the closest, most careful, attention are required if one is to escape this danger. Three criteria of essential beliefs may be distinguished: first, such beliefs will be minimal; secondly, they will be adequate; and thirdly, they will be consistent with one another.

By the first of these criteria—what might be called 'the principle of economy'—I mean the rule that theological beliefs, or, for that matter, intellectual beliefs of any kind, must always be the least possible; that one should never believe more than one has to. Earlier, and in a somewhat different connection, I urged that one can—indeed, cannot but—believe what seems true to one; now I am insisting that one must not —and in the truest sense cannot—believe more than this; that one has no right to believe what one is able not to believe; that unless truth *forces* us to believe it, we have no ground for assurance that it is the truth at all.

The recognition of this principle makes criticism not only appropriate, but absolutely indispensable. For *seeming* truth, as well as real truth, can exercise a coercive power. One may be in the apparent position, not only of being *unable to believe* what is really true, but also of *having to believe* what is really untrue. Both of these features of our situation may well be owing simply to our lack of knowledge: the first, to the lack itself; the second, to our failure to recognize it. We cannot believe truly because we do not possess the pertinent data; and we are constrained to believe falsely because we suppose we do. But the same results may ensue even when our knowledge is adequate, if we are not able critically to assess the facts and realities we do know and to discriminate between what is necessarily implied in them and what is not. And when we say '*necessarily* implied', we are saying that true beliefs, held with assurance, must, by definition, be minimal.

It may appear that in speaking so we are neglecting the role of the imagination in the intellectual life and forgetting that thinking may be creative as well as critical. Does not the mind, when things are as they should be, often 'play' with the data of observation and experience, being open to, and on the *qui vive* for, the heretofore undiscovered truth which will unlock their meaning, will justify, or 'make sense' of, them? And do not many of our most important beliefs, in every realm of our intellectual life, come to us as such imaginative apprehensions, or, as we more commonly say, in flashes of insight? The answer is obviously, Yes. In fact, it may be argued that a vital belief is never the product of mere induction, a simply generalizing description of actually known data. Our vital beliefs have their beginnings in imaginative leaps—generalizations which include the data but go beyond them. They begin as hypotheses, often exciting and glorious—*possible* explanations, *possible* justifications, of data which have perplexed or disturbed us. But though our beliefs may begin so, they are not truly our *beliefs*, or at any rate have no claim to be, until after they have been tested by the critical intelligence. We cannot know what *may* be true without including in our consideration all the possibilities we can imagine; but we cannot know what *is* true without excluding as many of these possibilities as we can possibly dispense with. Beliefs which we are justified in holding are the beliefs we are left with when we have tried, with the utmost honesty and with the greatest concentration of effort, to reject all of them.

* * *

Such a statement, although in the strictest sense true, might be misleading if the second criterion were not stated with equal emphasis: beliefs must be adequate. They must recognize and respect all the realities of experience and deal fully and appropriately with them. This requirement is not, strictly speaking, a 'second'; it is essentially involved in the first. For 'economy' implies inclusion as well as exclusion: what is kept must *suffice*. Beliefs are not really minimal if they do not cover the facts. But this second criterion deserves separate mention and emphasis because there is obviously more than one way of being intellectually dishonest and careless and, therefore, of being less 'right' than one can be. One may believe 'more' than the facts *allow* because one does not assess critically enough what they *demand*; but one can also believe 'less' than the facts *demand* because one does not allow sufficiently for the facts themselves. If we are sometimes too simply naive to discriminate the essential or necessarily implied truth in an experience of reality from what is merely apparent or fortuitous, we may also be not naive enough to have the experience at all—or, if we have it, not able or willing to allow, in our thinking, for the full range and depth of it.

This failure of adequacy, as the last remark will have suggested, is as often the result of a fault in our disposition towards reality, in our way of responding to it, as it is in our way of rationally understanding and interpreting it—although it is hard, if not impossible, to make a sharp distinction. This disposition or way of responding, far from being minimal or grudging, must be generous, positive and open. If we would know concrete reality, of whatever kind or under whatever aspect, we must be ready to let it speak to us fully and freely, to listen to it with heart and mind, to respond to it sensitively and appreciatively, even to go out eagerly to meet it. God's reality—to cite an example, the supreme example—even if it should be the 'realest' thing in the cosmos, would by definition be hidden from one who, for whatever reason, was not thus disposed. With regard, then, to our knowing of concrete things—upon which any possible knowing of *truth* is based— the 'principle of economy' seems inappropriate and, except in a minor degree, inapplicable. Indeed, the contrary principle, what might be called a 'principle of maximal exposure and trust', would seem to be the appropriate rule.

William James' phrase, 'the will to believe', is, I should say, more concerned with the indispensability of this appreciative, loving, adventurous attitude toward reality than it is with 'belief' itself. In so far as James is making a valid point, he is saying, not that we can ever properly believe what we want to believe because we want (however much) to believe it, or even that our desires have anything at all to do with determining what is true, but rather, that in order to be in a position to believe truly, we must be fully open to, eagerly responsive to, the creative reality we are seeking to understand—so much so as to be ready even to *act* on the basis of a tentative understanding of it with the hope that such action will lead to a fuller and surer knowledge. This openness and responsiveness are, to a degree at least, subject to the will; and true beliefs must take full account of what, in such moments or moods, is revealed to us. But this is far from saying that true beliefs themselves can be 'willed'.

I have just said that true beliefs must take full account of reality, or aspects of reality, revealed to us in certain *moments or moods*; and this requirement is so frequently neglected in our practice that it deserves perhaps a special emphasis. The problem, where it exists, does not lie in our failure to give due weight to such revealing experiences in the moment when they are occurring. In that moment we are fully convinced, not only of the reality of the experiences, but also of their being experiences of *reality*. The problem consists in our tendency to forget, or to distrust, or unduly to discount, the 'yield' of such experiences when, in more reflective and critical mood, we undertake to formulate our beliefs. We tend to assume that the only reality to be accounted for is the reality we steadily and constantly see or, as in scientific experiment, control the conditions for seeing; that, almost by definition, anything of which we have only occasional glimpses—and even these not of our contriving—cannot be real. This assumption is gratuitous and false. Occasional or momentary visions may stand in special need of criticism and testing, but they cannot be rejected out of hand as mere fantasy.

The same thing can be said—and this is a point even more important and pertinent—about visions of reality peculiar to members of various classes of men or even to individuals. I may, and should, suspect the validity of an experience, even a frequent or continuous experience, which, so far as I know, I alone have; but I have no right to deny its validity *a priori*. And when I learn, if I do, that to many others also, the world, or something within it, makes itself concretely known in the same way as to me, my confidence in the reality of what I have seen is bound to be increased, and ought to be—although it is still in need of rigorous testing.

Classes or groups of men who can be credited with seeing reality in distinctive, but possibly valid, ways are not limited to those who possess in common some peculiar capacity or sensitivity—as, for example, children and poets may—or even to those who experience in common some status or relationship, such as, let us say, marriage or parenthood. It is obvious that there are such classes of individuals and that reality or some part of it may make itself known to them in ways in which other persons simply cannot know it. But the same thing can be said of historically or culturally determined classes of men. We are so accustomed, in the modern age, to emphasizing the limiting effects of historical conditioning—which are very real —that we may not be as ready as we should be to recognize its creative and revealing character. Because I am, let us say, a Frenchman, I see or feel the reality of the world in a somewhat different way from that in which the Chinese or the Greek may feel or see it—and this fact may become the basis of a false pride and a divisive, destructive intolerance—but it may still be true that the incalculably rich reality of the world has in fact a character or aspect to which the Frenchman is peculiarly sensitive. In a word, we have no right to limit the concrete reality of which our beliefs must take account to reality which is equally accessible to all men. Once we recognize that concrete reality (as distinguished from abstract truth) always *reveals itself*, we cannot set limits to the times and seasons of this revealing action, whether in individual experience or in history.

Actually, of course, our experiential knowledge of reality and our beliefs about it cannot be entirely separated, because it is the same person who is both the experiencer of reality and the believer of truth. Moreover, he cannot keep the two roles apart. Obviously, he is thinking as he experiences and continues to experience as he thinks. But there may be differences in emphasis and proportion; and the two operations, although they overlap, so to speak, can be distinguished. And if it is true that one may miss the truth about a reality because one is unable or unwilling to *think*, it is also true that one may miss the reality itself because one is unwilling or unable to *listen*, and to remember what one hears. It is, however, about our beliefs, and thus our *thinking*, that we are just now principally concerned; and nothing said about the necessity of openness to reality contradicts the earlier emphasis upon the necessity of 'economy' in our believing. The true believer will believe what he *has* to believe, so long as he is fully open to, and takes fully into account, all the pertinent data. This means—to bring the discussion back to our particular theme—that beliefs implicit in, or necessarily presupposed by, Christian experience in its full concrete reality must be faithfully regarded as essential Christian beliefs, but that we must be equally faithful in recognizing as non-essential, if not untrue, any beliefs which cannot be thus described.

*   *   *

We are less likely to violate 'the principle of economy' as thus defined if we keep in mind the third criterion—namely, that of the wholeness and consistency of truth—recognizing that one cannot have identified truly an 'essential belief' if it is incompatible with other beliefs firmly and surely established in any area of our knowledge. We may as Christians find ourselves believing what, if we were not Christians, we would not believe (because we should have no adequate ground for doing so); but we cannot as Christians believe what, if we were not Christians, we should truly know to be false.

If, then, trying to be as 'economical' as I can be, I formulate a belief as 'essential' and then realize or discover that it conflicts with some surely established fact in nature or history, I must recognize that I have not been 'economical' enough. I am manifestly mistaken in supposing that the belief is really implied in Christian existence—mistaken either because I have not known, fully enough, the concrete reality of the existence, or because I have not discerned, accurately enough, its essential character and structure, or because I have not identified, strictly enough, the truth which is actually and necessarily implicit in it. On the other hand, if any statement from any source about things in heaven or earth constitutes, either explicitly or implicitly, an *inescapable* denial of truth *necessarily* implied in Christian existence, the Christian is bound to reject that statement as untrue. Such a statement, if made within the Church, is the 'heresy' defined in the first chapter of this book.

If one is wise in one's attempt to be 'economical' and 'adequate'—to identify *all* the essential, but the essential *only*—one will try to take into account, not only facts in nature and history which are already 'surely established', but also facts which may conceivably become such. The theologian will suspect that he has not been sufficiently 'economical' if he finds himself formulating a belief with which some yet-to-be-discovered fact may possibly conflict. To say this is not to affirm a separation between theology and reality. On the contrary, it is to affirm a relationship so close and complete that no discrepancy between the two can be allowed at all, even as a possibility.

I cannot hope to be altogether faithful to these principles; but I very much want to be, and intend to be, as we turn now to the application of them in several of the areas of Christian belief.

Chapter 4

THE CHURCH AND CHRIST (I)

IN the first two chapters of this book some effort was made to describe—or to recall—the concrete reality of the Christian existence; and the conviction was expressed that the basic Christian belief is the belief that what this existence necessarily presupposes or implies is true. The preceding chapter was concerned with proper method in determining what these necessary presuppositions and implications are. It remains to apply the method as well as I am able, and to ask what intellectual beliefs the inner existence of the Church requires—requires, not in the sense of making external demands or imposing external conditions, but in the sense of involving them as essential and irreducible assumptions—all the while remembering the point made near the end of the first chapter, that the beliefs will achieve any degree of precision more often through our rejections of the simple propositions of others than through simple propositional constructions of our own.

*　　*　　*

If participation in the Church is the first and basic element in the Christian theologian's responsibility and if the Church's theology is essentially an explication of the Church's existence, it would seem natural to conclude that the first object of theological thought will be the Church itself and that the basic Christian belief will be a belief about the Church. Strange to say, however, this is not the conclusion most Christian theologians have come to, if one is to judge from their works. Most 'systematic theologies' begin with God, move on to Christ, and finally reach the Church. Although I can make no claim to being a systematic theologian, I venture to dispute the propriety of this sequence and would maintain that in the appropriate order the consideration of the Church would come first.

The basic reason for such a procedure is the obvious one, already stated several times: to begin with the Church is to begin where we are and with what we know—that is, with what we know as Christians. The Christ we know makes himself known only there as the Christ he is; and consequently the God we know, being the 'God and Father of our Lord Jesus Christ', can be known only there as the God he is. The Church, in other words, is the concrete reality of Christianity. Christian worship is the *Church* worshipping. The Christian gospel is the *Church* proclaiming. Christian theology is the *Church* thinking and formulating. Moreover, the content of this worship and proclamation and the object of this thinking and formulating are provided by what is found within the Church's life. It is the actual being in history of this communal existence which alone constitutes ground, locus, and norm, not only for distinctively Christian experience and action, but for Christian thought as well.

In saying this, it seems to be that I am saying what is quite obvious; and therefore I have been surprised at the vehemence with which statements to this effect in other writings have been rejected by theologians for whom I have great respect. With what many of them affirm I can agree; but I do so without seeing that these affirmations constitute any refutation of the statement about the Church which I have just made. In a rather scathing review of an earlier book of mine—a review in which, if I may presume to say so, a number of gross mis-understandings of my position are involved—the writer concludes: 'The central question for faith concerns, not the accuracy of our memory of any historical fact . . . but the adequacy of our response [and here the writer quotes Schubert Ogden] to "the only 'objectivity' about Jesus of which the New Testament itself intends to speak, an *existentiell* communication demanding decision." '[1] Contrary to the reviewer's apparent supposition, I would not disagree with what he is asserting here, any more than with what I understand Schubert Ogden to mean. But, I would ask, where does this *'existentiell* communication' take place? And between ourselves and what reality? What is 'our response' being made to? Is it to some vision or word reaching us 'out of the blue'? Is it to something encountered in nature, in universal history, in our 'solitariness', or in human existence as such? Is it not clear that the *distinctively* Christian 'response' is made to none of these, but to a reality disclosed in a particular historical event (or, if you prefer, person) with which (or with whom) we have contact only through participation in a particular historical existence— namely, the existence of the Church? We may know that reality in an existential way only by participating, or coming to participate, in the *existence* to which it belongs. The 'communication' takes place there, and the 'response' is made there.

This does not mean that there can be no existential communication between God and man except in and through the Church. Manifestly there can be, and is. But if we are thinking of the 'God and Father of our Lord Jesus Christ'—that is, of God as distinctively known by the Christian—then, I do not see any way of escape from the conclusion that the 'communication' as well as the 'response' takes place in a particular historical nexus, within a particular historical body—namely, the Church—and that a distinctively Christian theology must begin with its nature and meaning.

[1] Everett Tilson in *Interpretation*, Vol. 17 (1963), pp. 466ff.

A second argument for such a procedure is really not a *second* argument at all, but only a restatement of the first. I mention it, and mention it separately, only because critics have sometimes made a special point of rejecting its truth. This 'second' argument rests on what, again, would seem to me to be the obvious fact that the *New Testament* begins with the Church. The New Testament begins with the Church for the same reason we do—namely, because it is what its writers immediately knew. They are writing, not only *to* the Church, but out of the experience of the Church. They know nothing Christian that has not reached them in this way. All their convictions about God, about Christ, and about man, in so far as they are recognizably Christian, are grounded in the Church's reality; all their theological beliefs are suggested by, felt to be implicit in, and explanatory of, this social-historical existence.

Can this conclusion be avoided? Is it not obvious that the Church's reality is the constantly present presupposition of the New Testament writers and that its concrete existence is the matrix of their thought? The same critic to whom I have already referred ends his review with the recommendation that I should turn to 'the Bible, to Paul the Apostle's discussion of the meaning of faith'. This I am glad to do. But having done so, I must ask my critic: What is the object of Paul's faith, how did the knowledge of this object reach him, and in what existential context did he possess it (or did it possess him)? Did it come to him as a light from heaven, without social or historical mediation of any kind? Paul himself may have thought so sometimes; but can *we* think of it so? And would even Paul have supposed for a moment that his faith, as he continued to live in and by it, was not a shared faith, possible of being his only because it was that of others, too—namely, the grateful, loving, and obedient response to God as he was experienced and apprehended in a communal life?

To be sure, we shall not expect the New Testament writers to be referring constantly to the Church, any more than we should expect an American writer, who writes as an American —whose Americanism indeed stands out conspicuously and unmistakably—to be fully and always aware of this character of his writing. Even if he were, we should not expect him often to speak of it. Ordinarily, we do not keep referring to what we take for granted even when we are entirely aware of it—and usually we are not. To suppose that one can refute the statement that the New Testament supports the view of the Church as the primary Christian reality in history by demonstrating (if one could) that its writers do not acknowledge, or even see, the fact of this primacy, is to make a judgment both unnecessary and untrue. The Church is obviously primary for them, whether they see it so or not.

But I do not want to be understood for a moment as making the concession that they did not see it so. I should say, for example, that Paul's basic idea as a Christian was his conception of the New Man. This New Man was not an individual but a new humanity—eschatological, to be sure, in its fullness and perfection, but, in its essential identity, actually present as the Church, the earnest of our inheritance, the very reality of Christ in history. It was from within this new humanity that Paul looked at nature, man and God—and, moreover, I see no reason to doubt, and every reason to believe, that he was fully aware of doing so.

*   *   *

In my attempt at the end of chapter two to designate the marks or 'notes' of the existential reality of the Church I included as one of them, 'the deeply-felt conviction that in the event in which the Church arose a unique and redemptive self-revelation of God was taking place and that in the Church that event is in a real sense constantly recurring'. I used the word 'con-viction' rather than 'belief' because I was speaking of the Church's *existence* and of the Christian's *existence* within it; and 'conviction' seems the more 'existential' term. But a 'felt conviction', even if it means more than a 'belief', certainly does not mean less; and the 'conviction' referred to involves a judgment of truth.

This judgment has to do with the actuality and meaning of an ancient event—the event which had as its centre the person and career of Jesus of Nazareth—and it is important that we identify this event correctly. It may appear at first that in naming Jesus we have already identified it. Certainly we have said something very true and important about it; we have indicated at what time and in what connection it occurred. Indeed, we may be said to have 'identified' it in the sense of designating it—of saying, '*This* is the event we are talking about.' But if by 'identifying' the event we mean defining its essential character, saying precisely what constituted it or made it the event it was, then we do not identify it when we simply point to Jesus; and I believe it is of the greatest importance for Christian theology, apologetic, and preaching that we should recognize this fact. Let me try first to demonstrate the fact itself and then to indicate why the recognition of it is im-portant.

The basic ground for affirming the fact itself lies in the meaning of the word 'event'. That term can, of course, be used in a very simple and general sense to refer to any occurrence or incident, no matter how inconsequential it may be. An example of this usage is our saying, 'In that event . . . ', meaning merely, 'If that happens . . .' We tend, however, to reserve the word for happenings of importance in some context or other: whether for decisive contests in an athletic meet, or for turning points in our personal or family experience, or for significant moments in the history of a people or of mankind. It is, of course, with 'event' in this last context that we are concerned.

Now, not only can it be said that significant moments, 'events' in this sense, belong to history, but also that history is made up entirely of such moments. Some happenings are more important than others, but every historical happening is important; otherwise, it would not be 'historical'. In so far as history can be analysed into its basic components, those components are events. Such a statement may be misleading because it suggests that the 'events' are in some way prior to the 'history'; that history is a combination, or aggregation, of already significant happenings. Actually, however, it is only within history that the happenings are significant. The 'event'-character of a happening is not intrinsic. The relation in which a happening stands to the whole social-historical context in which it occurs determines whether it is an event or not. An event, then, *is* an event only within the history of which it is, in a sense, both component and product. Only significant happenings belong to history, but only history makes them significant. The two—the event and the history—are thus by definition inseparable. The only content of history is events, but events have being at all only as thus contained.

To recognize this nature of history is to see that, strictly speaking, no individual, however important, can as such be 'historical'. For it would obviously be impossible to regard any individual as being, simply as such, an event. An individual may well be the dynamic centre or focus of an event. Such social responses may be made to him and such social consequences may flow from his words or deeds that an event can be said to have occurred and, moreover, to have occurred in close, and (so far as one may be able to see) in necessary, connection with him. But he himself will not be the event. The

event will be that complex concrete social occurrence, organic-
ally and inextricably related to other occurrences and therefore
beyond any possible exhaustive description, in which he played
a part. Still, however important, even decisive, his part may
have been, it is this event which immediately and intimately
belongs to history; not he.

For human history is a dynamic social thing—a vast social
happening—and the 'stuff' of which it is made has the same
dynamic social character. The emerging of new societies and
the changing fortunes of old, socially significant discoveries in
various areas of exploration and research, conflicts between
parties or nations and their consequences, influential literary or
artistic happenings or trends—in a word, socially important
actions, interactions and reactions, of innumerable kinds,
among persons and peoples—it is of such 'events' that history
is composed, and individuals in their solitariness 'figure' in it
only indirectly or, as it were, by reflection. However wise or
good or great they may have been in some intrinsic sense,
history 'knows' them only as participants in these larger social
wholes, which alone have historical significance or even
historical reality.

If all of this is true, it is clear that one cannot truly define the
historical event with which the Church's basic belief is concerned simply by referring to Jesus. We should thus have
named the event, but not defined it. Similarly, we use Napoleon's
name to designate an important event or cluster of events in the
European history of the nineteenth century, but we do not
define it so. And we may use Alexander's name in referring to
a turning point in world history—at any rate, in the history of
the West—but Alexander himself is not that 'turning point'.
This does not mean, needless to say, that both Napoleon and
Alexander, simply as the individuals they were, did not have
extraordinary qualities and abilities; and it surely does not mean

that they were not extraordinarily important in the happenings and developments we associate with their names. But they were participants in—one may even say, centres of—events; they were not events themselves.

Although the case of Jesus is in many respects incomparable, the same thing is in principle true of his relation to history. He belongs to history only as the centre of an historical event. He himself is 'historical' only in a mediated and, so to speak, derived sense. If he is more important historically than either Alexander or Napoleon, it can be only because the event to which he belonged was more important than that which we know by either of the other names, or else because he himself was a more decisive factor in 'his' event than the others were in 'theirs'. Actually, do not both of these reasons clearly apply?

What, then, *was* this event? I suggest that we cannot define it adequately and exactly otherwise than by saying 'the birth of the Church', the coming into being of the historical community whose existence we began by assuming. It is this community, its emergence and its fortunes, which belong directly and intimately to history. Jesus himself is 'historical' only as a figure—the central decisive figure—in this social reality. In other words, when we spoke earlier of 'the event in which the Church arose', we were not saying something additional about an event which could be identified otherwise, but we were actually making the identification itself and doing so in the only possible way. References to Jesus—his character, his teaching, his miracles, his death, his resurrection—will make up the largest part of any description, any phenomenological account, of the event, and as we shall see, some essential Christian beliefs are concerned with these matters. But if we are interested in formally defining the event itself, in identifying what essentially constituted it, is it not obvious that we can

do so only in the social-historical terms of the Church's beginning?

*   *   *

The statement with which this part of our discussion began was
not only that this understanding of the nature of the event is
true, but also that it is of the greatest importance for Christian
theology and preaching that it be recognized as true. We need
now to give some consideration to the grounds of this second
claim.

The fundamental one is that only if the event be identified in
the proposed way can the Church be sure that it happened at
all. We have spoken of a conviction, belonging to the existential
reality of the Church, of an event in which 'a unique and
redemptive self-revelation of God was taking place'. This
conviction necessarily implies an assured belief that the event,
whose meaning or effect is described, actually occurred. But
this belief can have no adequate ground unless the event is
defined somewhat as we have defined it.

For the Church can be sure of the actuality of the event only
on the ground on which alone it can be absolutely sure of
anything: namely, its own existence as the community it is. It
can be sure it exists as a community in history; and to know
this is to know that it came into existence. This is the only
happening in the past of which as Church it can be entirely
certain. As to when, where and how the happening occurred,
we cannot have the same kind of assurance. Except for two
basic facts about the event which, as we shall later see, are
'carried' within the Church's existence itself, these matters of
time, place and manner are matters of which the Christian can
have knowledge only on the basis of ancient documents and
other ancient sources and the researches of the critical scholars
who study them. Needless to say, facts, innumerable facts,

unassailably true by any appropriate standard, clearly emerge from this historical study. Indeed, most of the historical facts which have been traditionally accepted as true by Christians are fully confirmed by critical research. Still, in the last resort all such facts are known by hearsay—however confident, for all practical purposes, we may be of their truth. There is nothing in the existence of the Church which guarantees the actuality of any happening in the past not involved in its own historical beginning as the particular community it was and has continued to be. Unless, then, the event be defined in the way we have defined it—namely, as the birth of the Church—the Church can have no assurance that it occurred at all. Define it otherwise, and you make its occurrence an object, not of existential knowledge (which is another term for 'faith'), but either of credulous trust in some external authority or of mere inference, however probable, from documentary or other external data.

Even more obviously, if possible, the Church's assurance of the *meaning* of the event presupposes this way of defining it. This meaning can be expressed in a great variety of ways. The theological and devotional literature of the Church abounds in glowingly rich description: 'The dayspring from on high hath visited us to give light to them that sit in darkness and in the shadow of death and to guide our feet into the paths of peace'; 'God hath visited and redeemed his people and hath raised up a horn of salvation for us in the house of his servant David'; 'He hath delivered us from the dominion of darkness and transferred us to the kingdom of his beloved son'; 'For it is the God who said, "Let light shine out of darkness" who hath shone in our hearts to give the light of the knowledge of the glory of God in the face of Christ.' These are only a few of scores of passages from the Church's earliest writings which might be quoted; but surely no more are needed to remind us of the transcendent and radical meaning found in the event. It represented nothing less than the medium or locus of God's saving action for all mankind—a new beginning for human history, a new Creation: 'God was in Christ.'

Nor are we left in doubt of what God was understood to have been doing there, of what the 'saving action' was: he was 'reconciling the world to himself'. Here, again, if it were needed, one might quote innumerable passages. The 'darkness' from which man needs 'deliverance' is his selfish aloneness, with the consequent hostility and fear, not only towards others, but also towards life itself (that is, towards God). The Latin word for 'salvation' is also the word for 'health'; and 'health' means wholeness and peace—wholeness and peace which can exist within an organism only because the organism is itself fully at home within a larger whole—indeed, within that ultimate whole, which is God's world itself. Man's need, then, is at-homeness—and this means a love strong enough to overcome his own selfishness, to unite him in one body and one spirit with all his fellows, and thus to bring that at-oneness ('atonement' in its original sense), within and without, which is life and peace, health and power. The earliest Christians believed that in an event which they themselves had witnessed God had filled this need. He had, literally, 'poured out his Spirit [that is, himself] upon all flesh'; he had given himself to men and had thus, not only *disclosed* his love, but 'shed it abroad in [their] hearts', set it moving in the world, created a new kind of human community, a fellowship of that same love, a family of sons. The fulfilment of this loving purpose, which included all mankind, was still in the future—indeed, lay beyond the end of history—but the lively hope of this eschatological salvation was based firmly upon the realization that the purpose not only had been unmistakably disclosed, but was also being effectually accomplished.

But what was this 'event' in which this saving, liberating, reconciling action had taken place? And how could the Church be so sure that the event had this transcendent and creative meaning and value? Does not the only possible answer to the second of these questions involve as part of itself what we have just seen to be the only possible answer to the first? The Church's assurance that a divine reconciling act had occurred in history was grounded entirely in its knowledge of itself as a divinely reconciled and reconciling community. Its confidence that God's love had been poured out was based entirely on the fact that it had been 'poured into [*their*] hearts'. Its confidence that God's Spirit (another way of referring to his love, that is, himself) had been given was only its recognition of the Spirit's self-authenticating presence in the common life. And if the event is by definition that historical happening to which this kind of meaning belonged, can it be precisely referred to otherwise than as the event of the Church's birth?

The fact that the actual Church has always lacked so much of being fully and faithfully the community of the Spirit does not negate the accuracy of this reference. In so far as the Church is thus lacking, it is simply falling short of being the Church in the fullest, most authentic, sense. Its awareness of the Spirit is its awareness of its own reality and vitality, just as its awareness of its own reality and vitality is its awareness of the actuality and meaning of the event. In the complete absence of the realized presence of the Spirit, there would be no ground whatever for affirming either the existence of the Church or the occurrence of the event.

But the converse is also true: In so far as the Spirit is present, the Church both exists in its authentic identity and knows beyond doubt that God acted in history to bring it into being. Others may regard the Church as one among many comparable societies and may believe that it can be exhaustively described in the same naturalistic and humanistic terms as they. The Christian is bound by his very life as a Christian to reject any such view. The Church is a divine community—divine in a sense in which other communities to which he may belong are not, except as they may be included in it. God acted in Christ for us men and our salvation, and the Church in its true character is the embodiment of this gracious and saving action.

Chapter 5

THE CHURCH AND CHRIST (II)

WHEN I planned this short book of eight chapters, it was my intention to devote separate chapters to the Church's beliefs about itself and its beliefs about Christ. But when it came to writing the chapters, I discovered, after several futile experiments, that I could not keep the two themes apart long enough or (even for a brief time) consistently enough to be able to deal with either. To speak of the Church in its true identity is to speak of the event in which it arose, the event of which Jesus was the decisive centre; and to speak of him in his true, and only important, identity as Christ and Lord is to speak of the Church, where alone he is known as such. A separation between the two, or even a distinction for purposes of argument or discussion, is, as I came to see, quite impossible. Christology and ecclesiology belong indissolubly together. The Church's doctrine of Christ is its way of stating its understanding of itself. And so, although holding to my intention of the two chapters, I have given them the same double title.

A second chapter is justified, however, because, although one cannot divide between the Christian's belief about the Church and his belief about Christ, distinctions, at least in emphasis, can be made within the meaning of the word 'Christ', which involve beliefs we have thus far had no occasion to discuss. We have seen that when we use the term, we may be thinking primarily of the historical event or of the historical community (and the preceding chapter has emphasized the fact that we must be thinking to some extent of *both*); but we shall also be thinking, and often primarily, of the man Jesus. And what the Church must believe about *him* we have not yet considered.

* * *

I have been insisting that the basic distinctive belief of the Church is a belief about the event in which it came to be; and that for its assurance of the actuality and meaning of this event the Church is dependent, in the last resort, not on documents or other similar historical sources, but on the existential reality of the Church itself. We do not need to look *behind* the Church, we have only to look *into it*, to see all we need to see as Christians—indeed, to see all we *can* see *as Christians* in any distinctive sense. But the existential reality of the Church, as we sought to analyse it earlier, includes two elements which themselves obviously imply some beliefs about historical facts lying 'behind' it—and these elements are as essential within its existence as any of the other elements, and the beliefs implied by them are as necessary, and therefore as legitimate, as any other beliefs. These two elements are a deep awareness of kinship with the Hebrew-Jewish community and a deeply felt relationship with Jesus himself. It is obviously with the second of these matters that we are now concerned. But the other and closely related theme is of such great importance that something at least must be said about it.

The awareness of kinship with Israel was referred to as a 'sense of being the people of God—the God of Abraham, Isaac, and Jacob—and therefore of belonging to the same history as that to which Israel belonged and belongs.' The 'sense', although it obviously involves or implies a belief about the past—namely, that the Church had its historical roots in Hebrew-Jewish culture—is just as clearly something more than a belief. We believe that we stand in a close and essential relationship with ancient Israel because we *find ourselves* as

Christians actually sharing in its life. To this fact all the devotional literature and practice of the Church from the very beginning till now bears testimony. The Law, the Prophets and the Psalms, symbols and carriers of the life of Israel, belong integrally to the Church's life also. The event of Christ, as the particular event it was, is inconceivable in any other context than that which a Hebrew-Jewish culture provides. This is true as regards, not only the event's factual content, but also its inner meaning. As has been intimated several times, the understanding of the event as a fulfilment of the age-old hopes of Israel belonged essentially to the event itself. The event *was* 'the event' in no small part because this meaning was found in it. The God of the Christians—the 'God and Father of our Lord Jesus Christ'—was not a strange new God, but was the God of Israel. It was because this fact and the apprehension of it constituted an integral element in the Church's nature that the early heresy of Marcionism, with its denial of Christianity's essential historical connection with the older culture, was so clearly recognized and so decisively rejected. Nor can that connection ever be denied so long as the Church exists.

One is tempted to reflect here upon the mutual distrust and separation between the two peoples which an awareness of this connection with full faithfulness to its meaning would have obviated—not to mention the unspeakably cruel persecutions, which give the lie not only to the Christianity of the persecutors, but to their humanity as well. One is also bound to think about what will be the final resolution of the relations between Christian and Jew. I am convinced that we shall some day be one people—in very truth a New Israel—united in a common worship of the God of Moses and the prophets and of Jesus and Paul. We shall all be Jews (by whatever other name we may also be called) and be willing to recognize each other as such. The consummation will entail a far greater liberality in both

Judaism and Christianity than either now possesses; but this greater liberty, far from being mere indifferentism or a loose tolerance, will be the consequence of a sharper discernment of, and a stricter fidelity to, what is essential in each community's life.

But these are matters which lie outside the limits of our present discussion. All I wish to say at the moment is that in the Church's historical connection with Israel we have a fact, which, although concerned with the past, is nevertheless a matter of existential knowledge and is therefore beyond the possibility of doubt by the Christian.

*   *   *

The second such fact is, we have said, necessarily implied by the Church's 'felt relationship' with Jesus. This was described at the end of chapter two in two phrases: 'a reverent and loving memory of Jesus' and 'an experience of the Spirit apprehended as being both God's immanent reality as love and truth and the continuing presence of Jesus as Lord'. To be a Christian means sharing in this memory and in this experience of Christ's living reality.

Now this sharing implies clearly and unmistakably certain intellectual beliefs about Jesus, and it is important to discern what those beliefs are, being careful to include everything that is essentially implied and equally careful not to include anything that is not. I should say that two beliefs, and only two are implied—Jesus' actual existence as the human being he is remembered as being ('full of grace and truth') and his resurrection from the dead.

First, then, we are forced to recognize as inescapable a belief in Jesus' actuality. I do not say his 'historicity', both for reasons touched on in our discussion of 'event' and, more particularly, in order to avoid any suggestion that I am referring to a product of the historian's research. Jesus' actuality is a necessary implication of the Church's memory of him. The possibility that he did not exist is simply excluded—excluded, not because the historians have demonstrated that he did exist (as they have, to the extent the existence of anything in the past can be demonstrated), but for far deeper reasons. It is excluded by the nature of the Church. If the time should come when the Church is convinced that he did not live at all, then it would have ceased to be the Church. In a strictly analogous manner, if the time should come when I am convinced that the persons whom I vividly remember as my parents did not live at all, I should have ceased to be myself. For the memory of my parents is constitutive of me—not in the same degree as the memory of Jesus is constitutive of the Church—but just as certainly and truly.

This does not mean that historical research into Jesus' life cannot make a contribution to the life of the Church, just as I do not doubt that objective study of my parents' lives could make a contribution to their meaning for me. But there would not be any final or really vital dependency, either on the Church's part in the one case or on mine in the other. I recall a time twenty years ago when my colleague, Paul Tillich, having been good enough to read a recently published book of mine (*On the Meaning of Christ*), said to me, 'I agree with everything you say in the book except for a few sentences'—which he went on to identify. The sentences read:

But, someone says, suppose that tomorrow or next day indisputable evidence should come to light that this [the life of Jesus] did not really take place? The only possible answer a Christian can make to such a supposition is to say, 'Such evidence will not come to light.' The community bears in its heart a memory of Jesus, and it is inconceivable that it should either modify radically the character of that memory or deny its validity. . . .

To speak so, Tillich said, is to deny to the historian a jurisdiction which belongs solely to him. Only the 'picture of Jesus as the Christ' is a matter of the Church's own intimate and certain knowledge. 'But,' I ventured to say, 'even if it should be granted that the "picture" is the important thing, would we not need also to recognize that an essential characteristic of that "picture" as it lies in the mind of the Church [where alone, it may be said incidentally, it does lie] is its assured *truth*? Is it not *that kind* of picture? Would it be the "picture" it is if it were not known to be true? And is not this knowledge intrinsic, belonging to the "picture" itself, as is the case with a remembered image?'

A few years later, in conversing with Rudolf Bultmann on one of the very few occasions when I have had that privilege, I spoke of this exchange with Tillich. Bultmann agreed with the reply Tillich had made to the question I have just reported: only on the ground of historical evidence was it possible to find objective truth in the 'picture'. But then Bultmann added a very significant remark: 'Except in the moment of faith'. In that moment, he went on to explain, you know that this is the picture of *someone*, that this is a true picture.[1] To me the remark revealed, if I may be so bold as to say it, the primary fault in Bultmann's way of looking at this matter. The phrase 'moment of faith' suggests, not only an *individual*, but also a

---

[1] I hope I did not misunderstand Bultmann. I feel sure I heard correctly what he *said*, and the meaning I saw in his words is in line with *my* understanding of his position as he has stated it in many writings. But I cannot pose as an expert interpreter of Bultmann and may be mistaken. If so, I ask his forgiveness for any misrepresentation and the indulgence of the many scholars who know his thought so much better than I do.

small part, a single instance or aspect, of that individual's experience. Presumably one may *now*, in a 'moment of faith', very surely know the fact of Jesus' actuality and in a later 'moment' know just as surely that one does not know it at all. Actually, however, Christianity is, and has always been, a cultural reality, not primarily individual and subjective, but objective and social. What makes one a Christian is not momentary experiences of one's own but a sharing in the constant experience of an historical people. Suppose that for Bultmann's 'moment of faith' we substitute the phrase 'life of the Church'. In such a rephrasing we express, it seems to me, what is true in Bultmann's and Tillich's contention, but without making Jesus' existence *for the Church* a matter merely of historical investigation. Everywhere else any 'picture' of Jesus, in order to be accepted as true, would need to be drawn according to the documentary and other evidence and would be no more certain than this evidence is conclusive; but this is simply not true of the Church's picture. That picture is incalculably richer than could conceivably be constructed by an historian as such, no matter how well informed and imaginatively perceptive he might be; moreover, the Church knows it to be a true picture in a way merely historical truth cannot be known.

This does not mean, I repeat, that historical research into the life of Jesus has no contribution to make. It does contribute enormously in any number of minor but important ways— confirming or correcting. But such research can never establish the existence of Jesus, if by that name we mean the particular personal reality the Church remembers and loves. And if it does not establish that person's existence, it does not touch the centre of the matter at all! It may establish (to the degree historical evidence can establish anything) that someone named Jesus actually lived and even that he was a man of extraordinary genius and goodness. It may establish the fact that he was born in a certain year or decade, lived here or there, said this or that, died under these circumstances or those. But it cannot establish the existence of the Jesus whose image we hold in our hearts. That being true, it fails at the crucial point. The significant thing, however, is that, despite this failure, the image itself remains undiminished and undisturbed. This is true because it belongs, not only as image but also as true image, to the very existence of the Church. The Church, then, must believe in the actuality of Jesus—and this means Jesus as the Church remembers him to have been—and is forced to reject as alien or heretical any denial or even any serious doubt of it.[2]

*   *   *

[2] The relation between this memory of Jesus and the results of historical research, and the independence of the former of the latter at all vital points, can be illustrated perhaps with a reference to a book now exciting considerable notice, *Jesus and the Zealots* (Manchester: Manchester University Press, 1967; New York: Charles Scribner's Sons, 1967) by S. G. F. Brandon of the University of Manchester. Its principal thesis is that Jesus was virtually, or in his sympathies, a Zealot, that is, a member of a revolutionary party advocating military action against the Roman rulers of Palestine. It has long been recognized that Jesus was put to death by the Romans as a presumed inciter of rebellion, a revolutionary (actual or potential), nor can it be denied that his teaching of the kingdom of God implied ultimately the supersession of every earthly empire. It was then, implicitly at least, a politically radical teaching. Moreover, as William R. Farmer (*Maccabees, Zealots and Josephus* [New York: Columbia University Press, 1956]) and others have shown, the great majority of the Jewish people in the time of Christ (and not just a small handful of 'Zealots') were 'zealous' for the liberation of Israel from the foreign yoke. It would be strange if Jesus had not shared in this yearning for the freedom of his people. But this is far from saying that he was a Zealot in the usual sense of that term. If the meaning of it is extended to include everyone who was 'waiting for the consolation of Israel', then all patriotic Jews would have been Zealots, and there is every reason to believe that

I have said that there is one other—and only one other—belief
about Jesus concerning which one may speak in the same way:
namely, that he arose from the dead. I say 'only one other' and
recognize that something at least must be said to justify that
implicitly negative statement before we turn to the resurrection
itself. One thinks of the many credal and confessional affirmations about Jesus which I am apparently excluding—his pre-

---

Jesus would have been among them. Cullmann's argument (*The State in the
New Testament* [New York: Charles Scribner's Sons, 1956; London: SCM
Press, 1963]) that some of Jesus' disciples hoped he might be a leader of
violent action against Rome, and joined him on the assumption that he was,
is more than plausible, and that Jesus himself was at times tempted to
assume such a role is at least possible. That Jesus, however, was in fact a
Zealot in the narrow, militant sense is, on the basis of a critical study of the
documents, not only not proved, but can be maintained even as a possibility
only by what would appear to be a very arbitrary selection and use of the
literary evidence.

But all such argument is, strictly speaking, beside the point I am concerned to make. My point is that Jesus is remembered in the Church as a
lover of men—that this image of him belongs to the very existence of the
Church. Statements about him—including statements about his political
views or affiliations—are tolerable (whether they are, on historical grounds,
accurate or inaccurate) so long as they do not imply a denial of the truth of
that image. If 'Zealot' can be defined in such a way that Jesus the lover,
whose character is reflected in our earliest sources, the letters of Paul, and,
less directly, in the Sermon on the Mount, could have been a Zealot, then,
from the Christian's point of view, the possibility is allowable; otherwise,
not.

Returning to the historical discussion, I am inclined to think a small book
by V. G. Simkhovitch (*Toward the Understanding of Jesus* [New York: The
Macmillan Co., 1921]) in which, as in Brandon's book, the career of Jesus
is thought of as having significance primarily in a political context, presents
a more defensible position than does Professor Brandon, although Simkhovitch's work would have been better if he could have had the benefit of such
researches as those of Farmer, Cullmann, and Brandon himself.

existence as a heavenly being, the decision that he should come to earth as a man, his supernatural birth, his miraculous deeds, his effectual vicarious sacrifice on the Cross for man's guilt, his defeat of the demonic powers. What are we to say about such items as these? Must they not be regarded as essential Christian beliefs?

I should need to answer No to this question. This does not mean that any or all of these items may not be matters of belief for any number of Christians or, so far as that goes, for all Christians; nor does my answer mean that they may not in fact be true. I mean only that they cannot properly be regarded as essential. They belong, I should say, to the story or saga or myth (the question as to which of these terms is most exactly appropriate can be passed over in this connection) which came into being almost at once within the Christian community to explain the meaning of the event. That the event had occurred and was the divine and saving event it was—this was a matter of intimate and sure belief which, as we have seen, must be judged essential. But the earliest Christians' *explanation* of just how or why the event had this character and effect—this explanation bears the marks, as any explanation of experience always does, of a temporary cultural orientation and must, in the nature of the case, lack this essential character. The event as its meaning was known in the Church does not require this explanation. Other 'explanations', different at least in detail, would be conceivable. Actually, no explanation at all is required. One might simply recognize what God has done in the event which happened around Jesus—he has 'poured out his love', he has brought the new Man into being—without trying at all to explain how he has done it. It would be most surprising, however, if the first Christians had shown such restraint. It was all but inevitable that they should seek and 'find' an explanation. But even if it should be granted that, given the cultural situation and the intellectual world-view of these Christians, the particular explanation they 'found' was likewise inevitable, this would not mean that it is true and essential.

The problem presented by the christological story is complicated by the fact that although it may not be a matter of essential belief, it has become on other grounds all but indispensable within the life of the community. For this story, originally created to *explain* the event, served also to *express* and *communicate* its concrete meaning and effect, its peculiar quality, and to do so in what would soon appear to be the only possible way; and this continues to be so, whether one finds the *explanation* true or not. The story, therefore, still has, and, so far as one can see, will always have, a necessary place in the Christian tradition and a certain kind of truth—the truth symbolic representations of various kinds can have.

One is not necessarily being dishonest, therefore, when one says, 'I believe,' in respect to items in the Creeds of whose truth in the ordinary literal sense one is by no means sure, if indeed one does not find them, taken thus, incredible or even unintelligible. But in this discussion, we are trying to restrict the words 'believe' and 'belief' to intellectual judgments of what is true objectively and factually; and if the words are thus used, although it would be rash to say the story cannot be believed, one is forced to recognize that it does not need to be. The Christian existence does not necessarily imply the pre-existence of Jesus, his miraculous birth, or his vicariously compensatory death. It *does* imply his actuality as the loved and loving man he was remembered as being. And it *does* imply his resurrection.

This last statement can be made, and needs to be made, because it belongs to the nature of the Church to know Jesus as *living*, just as it belongs to its nature to know him as *having lived*. To all Christians in all the ages and everywhere Jesus

Christ is a living reality—a personal presence—remembered and also still known. This experiential knowledge of Christ the Lord belongs essentially and inalienably to the existence of the Church. But, obviously, it implies inescapably the *belief* that in some way, however indescribable or unimaginable, the remembered human being became the divine being we know. This 'becoming' *was* the resurrection, and one who shares in the common life, the life of the Spirit, will inevitably share also in this belief.

It is worth noting that this relation between experience and belief is true, not only for the Church in its later history and current state, but for the earliest 'witnesses' of the resurrection as well. They had the experience of seeing Jesus after his passion, but they did not *see* him *come alive*. In other words, they experienced his reality *before* they believed he had been raised from the dead. This experience of his reality was the necessary basis of the belief. But, just as surely, the belief was the inescapable inference from the experience. And all of this was true, not only for the few to whom visual experiences of the risen and exalted Christ were vouchsafed, but also for the hundreds of believers by whom the Spirit was known as his presence.

Thus, as the existential memory of Jesus implies his actuality, so the existential knowledge of the Spirit implies his resurrection. Our inability to describe phenomenologically the resurrection 'happening'—indeed, to go further than simply to affirm the fact itself—does not in any degree or sense discredit this belief. For the resurrection is concededly a miracle, a wonder, a quite inexplicable thing (and one who *a priori* rejects the miraculous will *a priori* reject it); but one's acceptance of it is not the superstitious or credulous acceptance of an alleged happening in the past, but is the recognition of a 'given reality' in the life of the Church and a drawing from that 'given reality' of a quite unavoidable inference. The miracle we immediately know is the miracle of Christ's presence, and the miracle of his resurrection is its inescapable implication.

The Christian, as I have just said, will be unable either to describe or to explain the resurrection—indeed, to do more than merely to affirm the fact: 'He arose from the dead.' But he will find himself inevitably rejecting the 'explanations' of those who assume that only what can be 'explained' can be believed. He will reject any attempt to reduce the resurrection to a purely mythological 'event'—a mere item in a 'story' or in an imaginary, even if symbolically significant, 'picture'. He will reject the views of those who see the 'resurrection' only in the persistence of the memory of Jesus, or in the continuing influence of his moral example, or in surviving traces of the spiritual quality of his human life. Such simple explanations the Church will inevitably repudiate as utterly inadequate, and therefore as irrelevant and false. It will reject, because it must, any denial, explicit or implicit, of the actual present Lordship of the remembered Jesus, alive after his passion, for the reality of this Lordship belongs essentially to its own existence.

*   *   *

We believe, then, and must believe, in Christ—in Christ *as Event*, reconciling and saving, happening long ago within the context of Hebrew-Jewish history and perpetuated in the Church; and in Christ *as Person*, through whom and around whom the event occurred and who, as remembered and still known, is the centre of the Church's life. We believe these things, neither as the arbitrary dictates of some external authority nor as the conclusions of historical research, but as the inescapable implications of the Church's existence and of our own existence within it.

This chapter may appropriately end with some words

written long ago by William Law, but as applicable now as then because they are deeply true words:

> If you go only outwardly to work and seek only for an outward proof of the truth of the gospel, you can know it only by such labours and in such uncertainty as you know other matters of history and you are always balancing what is said for and against it. And if you come to believe it in this way, your faith will be held by an uncertain tenure and you will be alarmed at every new attack and frightened at every new enemy that pretends to lessen the evidence of the gospel.
>
> But these . . . are difficulties that we make for ourselves by neglecting the proper evidence of the gospel and by choosing to know it as we know other histories that have no relation to us or connection with our own state.
>
> The gospel is not a history of something that was done and past seventeen hundred years ago, or of a redemption that was then present and only to be transmitted to posterity as a matter of history; but it is the declaration of a Redeemer, and a Redeeming Power, that is always in its redeeming state and equally present to every man.[3]

[3] William Law, *A Demonstration of the Errors of a Late Book* (third edition, London: 1752), pp. 246 f.

Chapter 6

THE FATHER OF OUR LORD
JESUS CHRIST

IN all that has been said thus far, whether about the Church or about Christ, God's reality has been constantly referred to, and despite the justification of our procedure which was offered earlier, one may reasonably feel that this theme should have had first attention. Surely God—if there be God, and the Christian says there is—must be thought of as a 'prior', more basic, reality than either the Church or Christ, in whatever way those terms are defined. This last claim, needless to say, must be granted; and if the order of procedure we were following were the order of being, we should undoubtedly have needed to give first consideration to the meaning of 'God' (although how we could have done so I confess I do not see, if it were a *Christian* meaning we were concerned to state). But, as a matter of fact, we are seeking to follow an order of distinctively Christian *beliefs*, and in that 'hierarchy' the belief about Christ can make some claim to prior place. Our beliefs about God do not determine our beliefs about Christ; the reverse comes nearer to being true. To speak quite accurately, however, one would need to say that it is our life in the Church which gives rise to both beliefs simultaneously and in inseparable involvement with each other. But, even so, the 'God' in whom the Christian believes is 'the God and Father of our Lord Jesus Christ', and, 'no one comes to [that God] except by [him].'

*   *   *

The issue is confused for us because the word 'God' has meanings for the Christian which it has also for other men. The term 'Christ' is significant only in connection with the history of Israel and the Church. It is a distinctively Hebrew-Jewish-Christian term; and so also is the idea it stands for. But this obviously cannot be said of 'God'. Both as word and idea, this term has a broadly human provenance and currency; and any discussion of what the Christian means when he says he believes in God must take into account the human and all but universal meaning of the term.

This 'meaning' is not primarily philosophical, discursive, or speculative—if it were, I should not be venturing to speak of it—but is concrete and experiential. The word 'God' is used by the philosophers to designate a reality which many of them find they must either presuppose in their attempts to describe and explain the cosmos or else identify as one of its constituent elements. 'God' is defined as the 'first cause', or the 'prime mover', or the 'ground of being', or 'being itself', or the 'principle of concretion', or in other philosophical terms, according to the metaphysical or epistemological position of the philosopher. If what is being referred to in these various ways is indeed real, if it is truly and objectively *there*—as the Christian says it is—it is not surprising that philosophers, trying to see and explain the cosmos truly and objectively, should find themselves considering and speaking of it. But the Christian belief in God cannot be expressed in philosophical terms, and the 'God' the Christian believes in is not the 'God' appearing in any metaphysical account of reality.

The relation between the Christian and the philosopher as regards what the Christian will believe about God seems to me to bear an analogy to what we have seen to be the relation between the Christian and the historian as regards what the Christian will believe about Jesus. The Christian may be assisted by the historian or the philosopher, but he is never finally dependent on what either of them finds, nor is he adversely affected in any vital way by the negative conclusions of either. If it were possible for the historian or the philosopher to establish beyond any question that Jesus never lived or that God is not, this last statement could not be made; but this situation does not exist and, moreover, the Christian is unable to regard it as even conceivable. For just as the knowledge of Jesus' actuality belongs to the nature of the Church, so does the knowledge of God's reality. Both Jesus and God are concretely known—the one as remembered in the communal life, the other as actually found, or as actually finding us, there.

But here the difference just now referred to is again apparent: concrete knowledge of Jesus is not possible except in or through this historical communal existence; but, quite manifestly, no such limitation applies to the concrete knowledge of God. All men, whether they recognize it or not, have such knowledge. To be sure, the Christian man's knowledge has its distinctive character, for he will know God 'through Christ'—that is, as God is revealed in the historical community in whose life he shares—and this whole book (not this chapter only!) is concerned with trying to express and, to a degree, to explicate the content of this knowledge. At the moment, however, I am making what might be considered a prior point: namely, that the word 'God' designates a concrete reality belonging inalienably to human existence as such, to our experience of the world whether as participants in Hebrew-Jewish-Christian history or in some other—indeed, that this reality may seem to belong to our experience quite apart from our relation to history at all. Some attention needs to be paid to this universal meaning of 'God'—not because it is separable from the meaning of God in the Christian's experience, but precisely because it is not. We are considering the Christian's experience as well as that of every man when we consider it.

*   *   *

How shall this universal meaning be stated? When men of various religious cultures, or even of none, use the word 'God' with seriousness (that is, use it to express something in their own existence), what common meaning does the term have? What, for example, is the 'obsession' which Gamaliel Bradford describes as 'a keen, enormous, haunting, never-sated thirst for God'? When Francis Thompson tells of his flight from the 'hound of heaven', *what* is pursuing him? When Bertrand Russell cries out that the 'centre of [him] is always and eternally a terrible pain', a 'searching for something beyond what the world contains', what is this 'something'?[1] When Augustine said, 'Thou hast made us for thyself and we are restless till we rest in thee,' of whom, or to whom, was he speaking?

It is obvious from these examples—as though we did not know it well enough already!—that the word 'God' may have the most poignant meaning even for one who doubts or denies his objective reality as an actual being or existence. Bertrand Russell in the passage from which I have quoted, having spoken of 'something transfigured and infinite, the beatific vision, God', goes on to say, 'I do not find it, I do not think it is to be found, but the love of it is my life.' He speaks of the experience as 'like passionate love for a ghost'. Here is a confession of love for God as real and sincere as the love expressed in Augustine's confession, although Russell must confess also his unbelief. Even at this point, however, the difference between the two may not be as wide as it appears, because, I

[1] Bertrand Russell, *Autobiography 1914–1944* (Boston: Little Brown, 1967 London, Allen and Unwin, 1968), p. 96. See also pp. 36 and 121.

dare say, Augustine, too, might say of God's reality, 'I do not find it.' It belongs to the nature of God that he is, as Russell says, 'not to be found'. If he were 'findable', he would not be God. That is as true for the believing, as for the unbelieving, lover.

But the full extent of the agreement between the two—and therefore the unique and universal meaning of 'God' in human experience—appears only when a further fact is recognized: God is also *ineluctable*. If it belongs to his nature that he cannot be found, it also belongs to his nature that he cannot be evaded. And *this*, one must say, is as true for the unbelieving, as for the believing, lover. The God who eludes us also haunts us (like Russell's 'ghost') or pursues us (like Thompson's 'hound'). We say, 'O that I knew where I might find him,' and, almost in the same breath, 'Whither can I flee from [his] presence?' When Russell speaks of the futility of his search for God and Thompson of the futility of his flight from God, they are speaking out of the same experience. For when we are aware of God, we are aware of him as the One whom we cannot find but from whom we cannot escape. Nothing is more characteristically, even essentially, true of God than this. It is thus we recognize him as God. It is because we have this experience that we use the word at all.

It is the fact that God is the undiscoverable One and the inescapable One which, more than anything else, makes man's experience the mixed and contradictory thing it is and accounts for the peculiar anxiety of human living. If God were simply undiscoverable, we should simply forget him, or better, we would never have thought of him, and thus would escape the acute and overwhelming sense of life's critical importance, the feeling of being under awful and incalculable responsibility, of having to choose perpetually between possibilities of infinite significance, of standing constantly on the verge of either hell or heaven, of either utter and final defeat or utter and final victory—in a word, we should escape much of the peculiar torment of human living. On the other hand, if God were simply inescapable, again we would simply forget him, or better, would never have thought of him (for we are as indifferent to what we know too well as to what we do not know at all), and again would have been spared the perpetual and desperate conflict of doubt and faith, of fear and hope, upon the issue of which the whole meaning of our life seems to depend. But the fact is that though we cannot really know God, we cannot forget God; though we cannot find him, we cannot escape him; though we cannot lay our hands on him, his hand will not let us go.

Alfred North Whitehead's book *Religion in the Making* is most important for its presentation of a metaphysical description of reality and of a definition of God in terms of that description. It falls outside the purpose of this book to discuss such matters, significant as they are; and I lack the learning and skill to discuss them adequately in any case. But the metaphysical description and definition can have the great value they have, and can make so impressive a claim to truth, in large part because of Whitehead's authentic grasp of the concrete and experiential realities with which religion of every true kind is concerned. The book is full of penetrating and illuminating comments on the religious life itself—that is, on what 'God' means in our *experience*.

At one point, he writes: 'Religion . . . runs through three stages, if it evolves to its final satisfaction. It is the transition from God the void to God the enemy, and from God the enemy to God the companion.'[2] The author does not explain or develop this statement in any systematic way, and I cannot presume to say with precision what he meant by it. I feel sure,

[2] *Religion in the Making* (New York: The Macmillan Co., 1926), pp. 16f.

however, that he did not have in mind a merely chronological
sequence between 'void', 'enemy', and 'companion' as ways of
apprehending God's reality, as though each 'way' ceased when
the next began.[3] As a matter of fact, I cannot help seeing a
correspondence between the first two 'stages' in this 'transition'
and the two quite simultaneous and inseparable—indeed, in a
sense identical—ways of knowing God's reality which we have
been discussing. 'God the void' is a way of referring to the
Object of our futile searchings; 'God the enemy' is a way of
referring to our implacable Pursuer. God makes himself known
to us as both in one moment of revelation.

And what, according to this way of understanding Whitehead's statement, is meant by 'God the companion'? I suggest
that this stage, when realized—or in the measure in which it is
realized, for it can never be realized perfectly—this 'stage'
means a free and inward capitulation to the 'enemy', an
allowing oneself to be captured, a giving way to the God
who seeks us. This is the stage of 'final satisfaction' because
we discover in that moment of surrender that the God who
seeks us is also the God we seek; that in being found of God
we find God in the only way God can be found; that in
being thus defeated, we are in the only possible way victori-
ous.

And must it not also be said about this 'stage' that although,
as we have seen, the experience of 'God the void' and of 'God
the enemy' does not necessarily imply, for the experiencing

[3] I say this despite the fact that Whitehead may be speaking of an historical
series primarily. The title of the chapter in which the passage appears would
suggest this, although, it seems to me, the immediate context does not.
Other attempts to find an existential meaning in these words can be cited.
See H. N. Wieman, *The Wrestle of Religion with Truth* (New York: The
Macmillan Co., 1927), pp. 3ff., and W. N. Pittenger, *Process Thought and
Christian Faith* (New York: The Macmillan Co., 1968), pp. 37ff.

person himself, assurance of God's reality in any positive and
non-subjective sense, the knowledge of 'God the companion'
does inevitably involve such assurance. One may persist in
doubting the reality of what one cannot help seeking or fleeing
from, but one can scarcely doubt the reality of what one knows
oneself to be possessed by.

It would be a mistake, however, to suppose that this 'final
stage' supersedes the other two in the sense of replacing them.
God is still, in a sense, the 'void' and he is still, in a sense, the
'enemy'. We still do not 'find' him, and he still 'pursues' or
'haunts' us, however poignantly aware we may be of his
nearness to us and of his loving purpose towards us. The
knowledge of God is thus no simple thing. He is at the same
moment most near and most far. He is the least adequately
and the most intimately known reality in our experience:
least adequately known, because, however sensitive we may be,
we cannot know God except as he touches us, and the great
ranges of God's being lie beyond our knowing; most intimately
known because his reality encloses us on every side and per-
vades our very being, and though in our dullness of mind
and heart we may not always know it, we cannot move
or stay without touching him. But this knowledge is not
familiarity; it is not contentment. The peace of God is no
simple complacency, however devout. It 'passes understanding', because it consists, not in knowing and possessing,
but in being known and possessed by One who entirely
transcends our power either to possess or to know.

In this experience of God in all three of its stages, his reality
is that of the Fulfiller of existence, rather than being (as is likely
in our more abstract thinking about him) the Ground of it, or
the Creator of it, or, as some would say it, the decisive Factor
in its creation. He reveals himself in our experience, not as
having made us, but as making us whole; not as the Beginning,

but as the End. The 'void' is a present emptiness needing to be *filled*; the 'enemy', an existing anxiety needing to be *healed*; and it is to our actual partialness, brokenness and loneliness that the 'companion' makes answer. But although the religious man (who is universal man at one—indeed, the deepest and most essentially human—level of his existence) does not find in his experience of God's reality (even of 'God the companion') the answer to his more abstract questions about the origin and nature of the cosmos, he will know inevitably and surely that the ultimate answers to these questions lie, not in anything he will discover, but in the transcendent reality which has revealed itself to him. The One who has made himself known as the End of existence must be the Beginning and Ground of it also. The transcendent reality and intimate presence, who is for us the Fulfiller of life, must also be in some way, however far beyond our ability to comprehend or define, its Creator as well.

*   *   *

Thus far our discussion of the experienced reality of God has proceeded without any reference to Christ or the Church. This does not mean, however, that we have not been talking about the experience of the *Christian*. As I have said earlier, my point is that the Christian's experience of God is to a large degree shared with other men; and I have been trying to indicate the character and range of this common human element. Even so, there will be readers of the preceding paragraphs who will judge that I have been speaking more specifically as a Christian than I have professed to do, and that there may be many men, even large bodies of men, who would not recognize as theirs the experience I have been describing or, at any rate, would not find the terms I have used appropriate. This may well be true. I am a 'birthright' Christian and, with the possible excep-

tion of Judaism, know from within or with any real sensitive-
ness, no other religious culture. The individuals to whose
experience I have happened to appeal—Augustine, Whitehead,
Russell, and others—are also sons of Western Christendom
and, whether they know it or not, belong in one degree or
another to the Church and speak out of its life. Maybe, then,
it is true of them and of me that what has been said about God's
reality bears the special marks of the Christian man's experience
to an extent we may not suspect. But in so far as this is true, the
fact merely supports and emphasizes the major point of this
book—namely, the priority of existence to belief and the
distinctiveness of the Christian existence.

For in whatever way the common character of men's
experience of God should be identified or described—or
whether any one person can conceivably be in a position to
identify or describe it—there can be no question but that his
reality is experienced in a distinctive way within the Christian
Church. I do not say in a superior or a more authentic way.
(I may be unable to avoid thinking this, but I cannot affirm it
as an objective fact.) The *distinctiveness*, however, is un-
questionable. The Christian 'feels' the reality of God in a special
way. He will not be able to reduce this special way to a verbal
statement. He may say, 'God is love,' or 'God is truth.' But
others may make these statements, too. Everything will
depend on what the words 'love' and 'truth' concretely mean
to him in that connection, and this he will not be able to say.
For what he will be referring to is an *experience* of God's
reality which he has as a member of a particular historical
community, and the peculiar quality of that experience cannot
be expressed in abstract terms, or, indeed, exhaustively or
precisely expressed in terms of any kind. One may designate
it, or point to it, by using such a phrase as 'the God and Father
of our Lord Jesus Christ', but one is not thus describing it or

distinguishing its special character. One must simply say that for the Christian 'God' is the transcendent Reality and immanent Presence, of whom we have been speaking, as this Reality and Presence are realized in the community which remembers Jesus and knows him as Lord—a Reality and Presence evoking responses of adoration, thankfulness, obedience, trust, and love which are peculiarly its own.

We are obviously recognizing here a special revelation; but, it is important to note, not a 'special revelation' as distinguished from a 'general' one. The distinction is, rather, between it and other 'special' revelations. For every revelation, I should say, is 'special'. In so far as it is given us to know God, the knowledge is given us, not as men in some hypothetical 'general' sense, but as the particular men we are. One cannot be a man in a 'general' sense; one is a particular man, living in a particular time and place, the product of particular historical and cultural influences, the subject of particular natural and social conditions. In responding to anyone or anything in our environment, we do not first respond 'simply as men' and *then*, in ways reflecting our own particular character and experience. Our response from the beginning is our own. One's response may in certain respects resemble that of all other men, however different their situations, but this 'general response' has no real being; it is an abstract generalization from many particular responses, both individual and communal, which alone are real. Far, then, from its being true that there is only one special revelation of God, or none at all, there are as many special revelations as there are individuals and great cultural groups of men for whom the word 'God' has concrete meaning—and even for many who do not use the word at all, for the mysterious transcendent Reality we have tried to indicate with the words 'void', 'enemy', 'companion' can be known without being called 'God' or by any other name.

But among all these revelations a particular one can be clearly and certainly identified as having been made in the Christian community. I repeat that I have no interest in trying to demonstrate the superiority of this 'special' revelation to all other 'special' revelations and would not know how to do such a thing if I were disposed to try. (How shall I compare what I know with what I do not know?) I am interested only in affirming the existential reality and therefore the uniqueness of it. To belong to the Church 'in spirit and in truth' is to be grasped by 'the God and Father of our Lord Jesus Christ'—a divine Reality which by definition is known only through the historical event of which Jesus was the centre and therefore only in the Church, where alone the event has continuing being and Jesus himself is remembered and still known.

I have said that no formula or proposition can convey the peculiar quality of this experienced reality of God. (Actually, of course, no formula or proposition can convey the peculiar quality of anything.) We may in some degree *express* its meaning in holy living and holy dying and in forms of art, but we shall not succeed at all in defining or even describing it. One can only confess it, adore it, love it, serve it. In our confessing and adoring, we shall, needless to say, use words, but the words will be 'pointing' words, not defining words; and they will be intelligible only to those to whom some knowledge of the reality itself has been given or is being given. The scientists and philosophers, as we have seen, may be able to say some true and useful things about it, but the particular concrete Reality and Presence the Christian calls God, the 'Abba, Father' of Paul's ecstatic cry—this Reality and Presence they will not know unless they are, like Paul, 'in Christ'. And even then, they will know it, not as scholars or philosophers, but as the 'babes' Christ speaks of, and they will be as helpless to say fully and definitively what it is as everyone, Christian or

not, for whom the word 'God' has existential meaning, must
always be.

*   *   *

From the beginning of this chapter we have been discussing this
existential meaning and have made little, if any, explicit
reference to intellectual beliefs which may be implied in it. But
that such beliefs are implied has surely been clear. That God
is—that, for all the mystery of his being, his elusiveness of our
categories both of experiencing and thinking, he nevertheless
really, objectively, *is*—surely this belief is one of them. One
does not need to believe that God is 'a being' or that he 'exists'
(much will depend here on how these philosophical terms are
defined). No belief about God's metaphysical 'nature' is
involved. But a denial of God's reality—his reality in a full,
non-subjective, sense—the Church could not find true. This
point is so obvious that there would seem to be little reason for
making it were it not for the momentary currency of the term
'Christian atheism'. About that phrase one can only say that it
cannot mean what it says and apply to any actual intellectual
position, now or ever. A denial of God's reality is a denial of
the reality of the Church's inner existence, and therefore of
what the word 'Christian' essentially means.

The same thing can be said about any denial of God's
transcendence of mankind and the world. The belief in 'the
greatness of God' does not necessarily entail an affirmation of
his 'absoluteness' or 'infinitude'; philosophical statements to
this effect may or may not be true, but Christian experience
does not require them. Still, the idea of God, for the Christian
as for others, is the idea of One immeasurably greater than we
can conceive or imagine—One of whom we can speak only by
using analogies from our own deepest and most exalted
experience, but to whom all our analogies are utterly in-

adequate. Only so can he be thought of as the Fulfiller he is known to be.

If what was said earlier in that same connection is true, implied also in the idea of God is the belief in him as the Creator of man and the world. Again, one would need to deny the inevitability of any particular definition of his creative work. Did he create *ex nihilo*? Is creation to be thought of as God's primaeval action or as a continuous, and continuing, process in which God is the decisive factor? Answers to such questions may be found to the questioner's satisfaction in the philosophical tradition to which he may belong or through his own reflection (or may not be); but they cannot be said to belong to the idea of God itself, as his 'creatorhood' in some undefined sense can be.

The same kind of double statement can be made about his reality as Sustainer, as the principle or power of coherence in what exists—as being, therefore, in a real sense Sovereign. The belief that he is the autonomous Ruler of a fully and pervasively determined cosmos—a belief regarded as self-evidently true by some and as incredible by others—is not required. Believing in God does not involve one's either finding an answer to the problem of evil or denying its reality. But if God is by definition the ultimate Source and Fulfiller of existence, the conception of him as being meantime the Sustainer of it, withstanding and finally overcoming whatever would disintegrate and destroy it, would seem to be implied as well.

Whether all of these conceptions can properly be said to belong to the idea of God or not, they can surely be said to be implied in the experience of the Church. Therefore, although any number of different ways of explicating God's relation to us and the cosmos under these several aspects can be allowed, no statement which implies a denial of God's reality as transcendent Creator, Sustainer and Fulfiller of existence can be accepted as true.

Also false will seem any view of God which denies either the possibility or the fact of that initiative in human history which we have considered in earlier chapters—the saving action we have witnessed in Christ and of which the Church was, and is, the issue and the embodiment.

Equally incredible will seem any philosophical or theological statement about God which, in effect, denies the truth and validity of the characteristic response the Christian finds himself making to him or which reduces to a merely subjective phenomenon the presence of the Spirit, God's own responding to our emptiness and need. To say this is to affirm the 'personal' character of God's relations with us and of ours with him. No view of God which makes inappropriate our saying 'Thou' to him can be true. I do not say that we must affirm, as a proposition: 'God is a person.' Since we know so little about what it means, or might mean, to be a person, I can see no proper ground for asserting that he is *not* a person; but neither can we say that he is. Even so, implied in the very existence of the Church and the Christian is the belief that with God our relations are essentially *personal*. We adore *him*; we give thanks to *him*; we trust *him*. Furthermore, we are loved by *him*; we find ourselves embraced by an all-embracing love—and can there be love without the lover?—a love which 'passes knowledge'. As this last phrase suggests, our experience with one another does not provide us with categories or language to define or describe One who is so far beyond and above us, but we know that we are related to him as the persons we are and that he responds to us as the persons we are, and therefore that he must be in some analogous way *personal* himself. No philosophical or theological definition of 'God' which implies a denial of this conclusion can seem true.

In a word, below any depths we can plumb or any heights we can scale is 'the Father of our Lord Jesus Christ'—the God who makes himself known in the communal experience of Christ's Lordship. In this experience we find ourselves adoring him, glorifying him, giving thanks to him, trusting our lives to him, committing to him our very souls. But this cannot be without our also believing with our minds that he is *there*, and that he is worthy of all the adoration, love and trust he has evoked in our hearts: Immeasurably beyond us but as close to us as our inmost need; unsearchable, but the answer and end to all our restless searching.

Chapter 7

THE LIFE EVERLASTING

AMONG the marks of the existential reality of the Church, by which all our beliefs as Christians are required and therefore justified, was included 'the confident expectation that God's true and loving purpose for his creation, "the uniting of all things in Christ", will be fulfilled.' The content of this eschatological expectation (that is, an expectation whose realization lies beyond history and this life) can be expressed in other, and no doubt better, ways and can never be spelled out with any precision; but the expectation itself belongs necessarily and ineradicably to Christian existence.

The traditional and proper word for this expectation is 'hope', and from this point on I shall use this word. I did not do so at first because this term, in popular usage, has lost much of its true force, often meaning no more than 'want' or 'desire'; and I was not willing to risk being misunderstood on a vital point. The Christian's hope of the life everlasting is not a mere wish for it; it is a confident expectation of it. I am using the word in this sense when I say that this hope belongs to the very being of the Church.

That the Christian life has always been characterized by this hope scarcely needs to be demonstrated. Already prevalent in much of Judaism, it was fully and overtly present in the Christian community from its beginning. Many scholars would affirm that the community, under its most important aspect, was an 'eschatological community'—that is, a community bound together by a common *hope*, the hope of the early end of history and the inauguration of a new and heavenly order of being in which all who belong to Christ would share. The Church—again, under its primary aspect—was a proleptic, anticipatory 'instalment', the 'first-fruits', of this future existence, or (in Moffatt's inspired translation of a phrase of Paul's) a 'colony of heaven'. Other scholars may regard such an understanding of primitive Christianity as involving an over-emphasis upon hope, an ascription to the early Church of too exclusive a preoccupation with the future. But no one will question the presence and great importance of this element in its life. The New Testament documents and the writings of the early Fathers reflect it on almost every page and would be utterly decimated if all signs of its presence were cut out. And could not the same thing be said of all the devotional, and of most of the theological, literature of the Church in all the centuries since and in every part of Christendom? Indeed, so far as I know, it is only in our own immediate period that a 'Christianity' without this transcendent hope has sought to establish itself. It cannot do so. The Church without hope is as inconceivable as the Church without faith.

The hope, indeed, is the inevitable consequence of that experience of God's reality in Christ of which we have been thinking in all the chapters of this book and especially in the immediately preceding one. Actually, the phrase, 'inevitable consequence', strong as it is, does not really do justice to the closeness of the relationship: the hope could almost be said to belong to the experience itself. For if it is true that to know God in Christ (perhaps to know him at all) is to know him as the Fulfiller of our existence, it must be true that knowing him is itself expecting the fulfilment. Thus, to have faith in God is to have hope in God. Paul is recognizing this fact when he writes: 'Now abide faith, hope, love. . . .' By 'love' he means the 'love of God'—that is, God's love coming to us in Christ.

By 'faith' he means our existential response to this love, our surrender to it, our receiving of it in humility and gratitude. But is it not obvious—or at least it seemed so to Paul—that this love cannot be thus received without there being also the 'hope' that God, who has given us so much, will in the end 'give us all things'? We sometimes speak of 'these three' as the 'three [supernatural] virtues', but to do so is to fall short of recognizing their true nature if we are taking the word 'virtues' in its usual sense. Paul is constantly mentioning what may be called 'virtues' of the Christian life (all of them, from his point of view, 'supernatural')—patience, sincerity, kindness, joy, peace, self-control, and many more—but 'these three' he sees as essential ingredients of Christian existence in a sense none of these 'virtues' can be said to be.

To be sure, there are some differences in importance among them. Love, he tells us, is 'the greatest'; and if the love is God's love 'shed abroad in our hearts', his 'Spirit given to us', the initiating and creative element in all that happened in Christ, we can readily see that this is true. Faith, as our realization and acceptance of this love, is manifestly next in importance. Only in third and last place is hope. It belongs to the nature of hope that this should be true. For hope cannot have the same existential certainty as faith. When the Nicene Creed says, 'I look for the resurrection of the dead and the life of the world to come', it uses precisely the right phrase, it being understood that to 'look for' means not to 'search for', but to 'expect' or to 'hope for'. Moreover, the statement is a simple confession of a fact: we *find ourselves* looking for 'the world to come'; it belongs to our nature as Christians to look for it.

But even so we are *looking for it*, however confidently; we do not, cannot know it as we can know God (or can know ourselves to be known by him). But though hope is in third place, following upon faith as faith follows upon love, still hope also 'abides'—an indispensable element in the Church's life. The 'three' are inseparable and constitute together the basic structure of Christian existence. The Church will have ceased to be the Church when its characteristic hope is not there.

*   *   *

This hope is manifestly more than a belief of the mind, just as faith is more than a belief of the mind. In each case, we are concerned with an attitude, a stance, an action, almost a state, of the whole person. Hope is a confident waiting and an eager looking, just as faith is an existential knowing and a sure possessing (or being possessed). And, as we have just been observing, it is important to recognize that life after death is the object, not of faith (as the Church, Christ, and God are), but of *hope*. Still, as there are necessary intellectual implications of our faith, so there are of our hope. And because the hope belongs as inalienably to Christian existence as does the faith, these implications constitute, as truly as the implications of faith, indigenous and indispensable beliefs of the Church.

At the very least, one must recognize the necessarily implied belief that the hope is valid—in other words, that the hope is in fact *hope*. We cannot 'look for the resurrection of the dead and the life of the world to come' without *believing* that there is, or will be, such a 'world' and that there is possible 'life' in it for such beings as we are. It is important to emphasize this basic belief because of the vulnerability of the Christian hope in the modern world and its apparent weakness in the contemporary Church. With reference to no other element in the Christian existence have what Walter Lippmann once called 'the acids of modernity' had so obviously destructive an effect. It is not surprising that this should be true. The modern secular age with its impressive achievements in science and technology is asking the Church to give up its life—not less!—and is exerting powerful and powerfully subtle pressures to force that surrender. Under this pressure it is not strange that, among the elements of that life, our hope should seem both the least defensible and the most easily dispensable. Only later, if we should surrender it (as actually we shall not), would we learn that in losing it we should have lost everything we have and know as Christians, for the hope of the life everlasting belongs integrally with faith in the love of the Father of our Lord Jesus Christ. As a matter of fact, it would be impossible to lose the hope if the sense of the reality of the Spirit and of the love of God in Christ had not already been lost.

But belief in the validity of the hope is meaningless unless we also have some beliefs about its object or content. May not one reason for the contemporary weakness of our hope be our failure to state, or even to try to state, *what* we hope for? We can rule out as utterly inadequate the views of those who would identify 'immortality' with the persistence of one's influence among one's fellows or with membership in what George Eliot called 'the choir invisible', noble and true as this conception may be. Nor can 'life of the world to come' be reduced to one's 'living on' (for a while) in the memory of others, or even to 'living on' (forever) in God's memory, unless the word 'memory' is being given in the latter case an entirely new meaning (as perhaps it can and should be). We find ourselves saying that we hope for the full vision of God, to belong fully to Christ, to share fully in the new life of the Spirit, to experience love in its full integrity and abundance—both loving and being loved. Such statements about our hope for ourselves and others are significant statements. But can anything more, or more definite, be said?

There is no exaggerating the difficulty of this question. Indeed, there is a kind of danger even in trying to answer it. One who ventures even a little way in the direction of fuller description or more exact analysis of what we find ourselves hoping for in Christ is almost certain to be led into false paths and to be lost eventually in a wilderness of unresolvable and ultimately irrelevant issues. One of the most striking features of the New Testament references to the life beyond death is their economy as regards descriptive detail of any kind. We are reminded in a typical passage (I Peter 1:3-5) that by God's 'great mercy we have been born anew to a living hope through the resurrection of Jesus Christ from the dead, and to an inheritance which is imperishable, undefiled, and unfading, kept in heaven for [us], who by God's power are guarded through faith for a salvation ready to be revealed in the last time'; but the 'inheritance' is being 'kept in heaven' and the 'salvation' is yet 'to be revealed'. The writer does not venture upon any detailed description of what is in store for us. The 'living hope', for all its own vividness and certainty, does not involve either a vivid picture or a sharp analysis of its object.

The same restraint or reticence (if such terms are applicable to what was certainly undeliberate and unconscious) characterizes Paul's dealing with this theme. No New Testament writer expects the life of the world to come with greater assurance and no one is more frequently occupied with that expectation (the word 'hope' occurs in Paul's letters around 40 times); but one searches in vain for any full or detailed description. Twice (Romans 5:2; Colossians 1:27) he refers to the Christian hope as 'the hope of glory'—perhaps the most adequate, and the least easily explicable, phrase one could find. Only the book of Revelation, which is certainly not typical of the New Testament, attempts to picture what this 'glory' may involve. But even this book offers no answers to many of the questions we may be tempted to ask. Such silence on the part of the biblical writers is bound to put us on guard against becoming involved in any rash effort to describe what lies 'beyond our bourne of time and place' and therefore beyond our power to conceive or imagine. Two things can be said, however, and I believe it is important to say them.

One of these has to do with the personal (for lack of a better word) character of our hope. God loves us as the selves or persons we are—here indeed is the profoundest meaning, the truest definition (the Christian would say) of either 'self' or 'person'—and the salvation we hope for in Christ is salvation as those same selves. This is certainly part of what is meant by the 'resurrection of the body'. No expectation of nirvana must be confused with the Christian hope. My brother's own life, my own personal life, will in its own distinctive integrity be brought to fulfilment. This preservation and enhancement of personal existence belongs essentially to our hope because it is essentially implicit in the whole ground of our hope, namely, in the new life of the Spirit in the body of Christ. In our actual experience of belonging to him we are not less free or less truly ourselves, but more. Can our hope, then, conceivably take any other form than the expectation that, when we shall have come *fully* to belong to Christ we shall also have become fully free and fully ourselves?

This does not mean, however, that the Christian hope for the individual is the hope of a simple continuation beyond the grave of his present existence. The life everlasting is not our natural life continuing by its own momentum, as it were, through the specious finality of death. Death is no fiction, no mere appearance. Death, according to every indication, is more than the death of the physical body; it is the end—the real end —of our natural human existence. There is no way of denying or minimizing the actuality of death, and the Christian hope does not involve our doing so. Indeed, that hope involves our taking death with realism and with utter seriousness. It is on this account that the word 'immortality' is used so seldom in the New Testament and has always been more than a little suspect.

For our hope in Christ is not the illusion that we shall not 'really die', but is the assurance that we shall die 'in God'; that God will not leave us in death; that we cannot drift beyond his love and care; that he who has given us a 'foretaste', a token portion, of a divine life will eventually bestow on us the fullness of it. In spite of all the evil which needs to be destroyed and the dross which must be cleared away, we cannot help believing that this divine life will catch up into itself our present selves, transforming them, but also conserving them in their true and essential identity. But the ways in which this will be done are unimaginable, and we cannot truly or adequately picture them in terms of our wish to see continued the familiar structures of the natural and human world, by which our present personal existence is so largely determined. God will make us what we were created to be and therefore what we most truly are. Whatever in our present conscious existence is essential to his doing this, and doing it to us, will be conserved. But we are not in a position to say just what this essential element is. And certainly our own finite human wishes—even our most un-selfish wishes—do not give an adequate clue.

This means, one must recognize, that we cannot truly hope for much that we may find ourselves wishing for; but it also means that what we have grounds for hoping for in Christ includes much more than we could possibly wish for. If our loving wishes for others or for ourselves in relation with others fall short of fulfilment, it will be only because the fulfilment will so far outrun them. God has in store for us more than we can ask or think; and this is true, not only because we shall have been brought into an unimaginable environment which will hold for us unimaginable possibilities of good, but also because we ourselves shall have been transformed, shall have become the selves whom God alone now knows us to be. To say that, thus transformed, we should not be 'ourselves' in any significant sense and that the 'everlasting life' being affirmed is thus reduced to irrelevance, is to presume to a knowledge of the mystery of self-hood which we simply do not have.

Objection is sometimes made to the belief in the resurrection of the self (however transformed) on the ground that the belief involves an exaltation of the self, an ego-centricity, which cannot be appropriate to the nature of things. Theists may make this point, even Christian theists; and it deserves attention. Is the Christian hope a selfish hope? The answer, it seems to me, is that it is not such, in its essential nature, although one cannot deny that Christians have often embraced distorted self-centred forms of it. The true hope is not: 'In the end, I.' It is not even: 'In the end, mine'—although it is worth noting that the human concern about life after death is almost always much more poignantly felt on behalf of loved ones than for oneself. But the hope is not truly expressed in either of these statements. The true phrase is: 'In the end, God'—which means 'In the end, love.' But if, as was briefly suggested in the preceding chapter, there cannot be love without the lover, neither can there be love without the beloved. If it is God's own purpose 'to bring many sons to glory', one does not need to be selfish in order to hope for its fulfilment. It is (or should be) our very love for God which moves us to want never to be separated from him, and it is our confidence in his love for us which alone makes of our want also a hope.

Appropriate in this same connection is the second belief spoken of earlier as clearly implicit in the Christian hope and in the grounds of it. This is the recognition that the fulfilment of the self of which I have been trying to speak will come to pass in and through community, and only so. Sometimes we find it necessary to say that heaven is not a place, that it is a state of mind. Since there is so much to indicate that space, like time, either represents only a necessary human way of thinking or, at most, a character of this familiar world of men and things, perhaps we are justified in denying that heaven is a place. But we are not justified in adding that it is a state of mind—that is, if we share the Christian hope.

Heaven is a society—a body of free persons, a community of free spirits. And since it is impossible that we should think of such a society in any realistic way except as occupying space, we are nearer the truth when we call heaven a place than when we call it a merely subjective state. Heaven is what we know, partially and proleptically, in the Church. It is the Church fulfilled, become fully its authentic self. Heaven is the divine community, whose life is its worship and whose worship is its life. It is God's love finally having its way, flowing without hindrance into our hearts and flowing without hindrance into one another and out of one another, creating among us—and this means, we find ourselves hoping, among all mankind (for how can God's love stop short of such an end?)—that unity in which alone each of us can freely be his true and complete self. Heaven is that full fellowship with Christ of which we have now only a foretaste; the full possession of an inheritance of which the Church is only an earnest; the full life of the Spirit of which we have received only a token. Heaven is perfect atonement, reconciliation, peace—to be realized within ourselves because it first will have existed within the new creation of God's love, of which, freed from all inhibitions and impediments, we shall have become a full and living part.

It is to such a fulfilment that we look. This is the 'glory' for which we hope and for which we cannot help hoping. We hope for it—and let it not be forgotten that hoping means, not mere wishing, but confident expecting—we hope for it, not because we deserve to, or can find adequate grounds for doing so in our natural human life, or can offer any convincing 'proofs' that such a glory is in store for us, but because God in Christ has already begun to give it to us. We hope only for what we have already begun to receive. 'We rejoice in the hope of the glory of God . . . for the love of God has been shed abroad in our hearts through the Holy Spirit which has been given unto us.'

Chapter 8

THE LAW OF CHRIST

THE final item among the 'notes' of the existential reality of the Church which I ventured to propose at the end of chapter two was 'the recognition that a distinctive way of feeling and acting toward all men (namely, the way of that same love) appertains essentially to the new existence and is therefore open to, and obligatory upon, those who share in it.' In other words, participation in the Church's existence not only involves an awareness of some present realities, a memory of some past ones, and the hope of a future fulfilment—all of these the Church's own—but it involves also an equally characteristic sense of obligation. The Church has its own way of sensing or feeling, not only what is, what has been, and what will be, but also what *ought* to be. And just as the rest of its distinctive sensing or feeling or experiencing necessarily involves some distinctive believing as well, so does its way of knowing the reality and content of this 'ought'.

I have referred to this characteristically Christian ethical awareness as a sense of obligation to feel, and in appropriate ways to express, what I spoke of as 'that same love'—meaning not 'love' in some abstract or general sense, but rather that love of which we have been speaking as 'God's love shed abroad in our hearts' and which, as experienced, cannot be distinguished from the Spirit. In the attempted description of the inner reality of the Church (to which this whole discussion has been constantly returning) I spoke of the experience of the Spirit as 'evoking a characteristic response of adoration, thankfulness, and love, and constituting a new and highly distinctive fellow-ship—a partnership in love of a quite unique kind.' It is the realization of *this* love which creates the distinctively Christian sense of obligation. The author of the Fourth Gospel describes it in his own authentic way when Christ says, 'Love one another as I have loved you.' And it is the beliefs or judgments which are necessarily implied by this sense of obligation which constitute the distinctively Christian ethic.

Now I do not propose to attempt any systematic analysis of this ethic (if that is possible in any case!); and certainly it is not my intention to consider the innumerable problems, theoretical and practical, which anyone who reflects seriously on the ethic, much less undertakes seriously to apply it, will confront. These, like many other themes similarly touched on in this book, lie outside its scope. Nor am I concerned to demonstrate, or even to claim, that the Christian ethic is 'superior' to other ethical 'ways'. My only purpose is to affirm its distinctive reality. Giving 'a cup of cold water in [Christ's] name' is not simply giving 'a cup of cold water'. A certain characteristic way of seeing what human relationships really are, and therefore what they ought to be, belongs essentially to the Church's existence.

This is true because the Church is bound to find this norm in its own life—that is, in its own true life. The Church is a 'colony', an advance token, of the humanity which ultimately will be. Its primary duty, accordingly, is to *be* what it is—the community of the Spirit, the community of the love of God in Christ reaching out to include all men. Its primary mission is simply to fulfil its own destiny—to be the constantly widening sphere of a constantly deepening reconciliation and fellow-ship. For the Church in its true character is not separate from humanity; it *is* humanity renewed in Christ, and its fullness will be nothing less than the healing of the nations.

The distinctively Christian ethic is thus primarily a *social* ethic—an ethic concerned with the character of society *as a whole* and with human relationships within it. By a strange perversion, this ethic has come to be, for perhaps the majority of Christians, Catholic as well as Protestant, a merely personal code governing the attitudes and behaviour of individuals towards one another. Often, therefore, the propriety of the Church's concern for changes in the basic structures of society is questioned and the concern itself is resented as though it were an alien element. Actually, however, not only is this concern not alien to the characteristic Christian ethic; it is at the very heart and centre of it. The Christian ethic is basically an ethic of social organism and structure. What 'Jesus came preaching' was the kingdom of God; and this is primarily a social conception. The consequence in history of this 'preaching', and indeed the issue of the entire event of which it was a part, was the Church; and the Church is not an aggregation of individuals, but is a corporate social reality, in principle and promise inclusive of all men, of all orders, nations and classes. There is, to be sure, a characteristically Christian obligation of person to person, but this owes its special character to the Christian's allegiance to the new humanity which, he believes, God has created in Christ. This social character of the authentic Christian ethic can the more readily be hidden from us because, owing to the political and economic weakness of the primitive Christian communities, not to speak of their vivid expectation of the early end of this world with all its orders, the New Testament documents have little occasion to speak of it. But this silence does not affect the basic and inescapable fact. The Christian ethic is primarily a social ethic.

To say this, however, is not to say that the Church's way of acting for the redeeming of the social order can be identified with, or reduced to the level of, secular movements for social reform or renovation, admirable as some of these movements may be. The Church's concern about the unjust and inhumane structures of society, in so far as it is authentically its own, belongs to its existence as the particular community it is and, on that account, is *sui generis*. The Church has its own way of being relevant to the orders (or disorders) of the world. It may not take this way, but there is no other way for it to take and still be relevant *as the Church*. Criticism of the social order which proceeds on the basis of merely humanistic premises and which is indistinguishable as regards its rational presuppositions and moral tone, its objectives and norms, from that belonging to some secular party or movement—such social criticism is in no sense or degree the obligation of the Church; and the Church which engages in it is denying its reality as Church no less certainly—although less shamefully—than the Church which is failing to make any judgments at all about the social order. This does not mean, needless to say, that Christians often, and sometimes even the Church corporately, will not find themselves co-operating with various secular parties and movements in social *action*. But the Church's *grounds* for this action will be its own, and these grounds will determine the distinctive quality of the action itself.

Because this is true in principle, and so often is not true in fact, I venture to suggest that where the Church's social criticism is resented and resisted within the Church itself, the reason may sometimes be that the criticism is not authentically and characteristically *Christian*. It does not 'sound like' Christ. It is not qualitatively consistent with the devotional life of the Church. In so far as this is true, it *is* indeed an 'alien element'. But it need not, and should not, ever be true at all.

*   *   *

Let me illustrate the point by applying it to the ethical issue which is just now of paramount and most poignant concern to

Americans and is increasingly becoming such to men everywhere in the West—the issue created by the prevalence of
racial division and discrimination. There is no need to speak
generally of the sinfulness and tragic consequences of this evil
state; I am speaking only about the Church's duty with
respect to it. Is it not clear that its primary duty is actually to
become itself the inclusive interracial community it must be if
it is to be truly the Church at all? If the Church is to have anything relevant to say about the evil of racial conflict, it must
speak out of its own life as a community of reconciliation. The
awful shame of the institutional Church, at any rate in America,
is that, by and large, it is not in this respect such a community
and therefore in that measure denies its own reality as Church.
The literally intolerable fact is that the Church is as much
divided in its racial constituencies as the rest of our society.
How incredible, how monstrous, that local groups of Christians
should call on the police to turn from their doors 'men for
whom Christ died'! But this is only the extreme instance of a
division between Negro and white Christians which cuts
across every body in Protestantism—yes, and for the most part
Catholicism also. How anomalous and how unspeakably
shameful! Does someone ask how the Church can become
relevant to the racial situation? Is not the answer unmistakable?
It can become relevant only as it overcomes the divisions of
race within its own life. It can fulfil its distinctive mission only
by becoming its distinctive self.

Many years ago now—so long ago that I believe it will not
be improper for me to speak of the incident—I was asked by a
committee of the Race Relations Department of the (then)
Federal Council of Churches in the United States to compose
the text of the 'Message' which the Council was to circulate
for reading in the churches on 'Race Relations Sunday' in the
coming February. (The present National Council continues

this practice.) I had often complained to the friend of mine who was then executive secretary of the Race Relations Department that it seemed to me the Council's 'messages', generally speaking, said what any group of believers in justice and humanity might say; that they were not in any distinctive sense Christian. And I suspect that I was being asked to write the message because I had made this criticism. Having found fault with others, I was being challenged to do better myself.

The Message I wrote was almost entirely concerned with the Church's own life. It spoke of the anomalousness of racially divided churches, the sin of racial segregation within the body of Christ, the rejection of the whole Christian position which was implicit in this separation of brother from brother. It asked how the Church could hope to bring peace when it was itself divided, or how it could presume to urge the nation to a brotherhood so flagrantly violated and denied, not only in the practices of its members, but in the very structures of its corporate life. It was, in a word, an addressing to the Church of a call to repentance and of a challenge to become the actual community of reconciliation we must be if we are to be ministers of reconciliation in this divided world.

My proposed 'Message' was rejected by the committee, partly perhaps because of defects in its format and style, but chiefly because its content was deemed inappropriate and inadequate. The chairman of the committee, in conveying its decision to me, pointed out that the Message did not say so many of the things which any pronouncement on race relations should say. He simply did not see that what it *did* say was the thing the Church alone could say and, moreover, the only thing there was any point in the *Church*'s saying. Others could say the other things quite as well. He pleaded with me to try again, saying that he had assured the committee that I could do a better job. Reluctantly I agreed, forgot that I was a Christian writing for the Church, and produced the kind of document which, with the exception of a few phrases perhaps, any believer in justice and humanity could have written. This was approved by the committee and was eventually read in the churches.

*   *   *

It is obvious that the Church's becoming the inclusive community of love it essentially is, involves much more than admitting—even welcoming—all men into its formal membership. May it not be said, indeed, that the principal reason churches often deny their nature by exclusiveness of any kind is the recognition on the part of their members that this 'much more' is involved? For to share with others in the love of God in Christ means more than standing with them at the same altar or joining with them in singing the same hymns or hearing the same Scriptures and sermons, or even sharing with them in the same experiences of the Spirit's presence. It means the opportunity, and obligation, to share all our privileges and, if needed, our goods with them. It means recognizing and opposing those social structures which condemn them and their children and neighbours to intolerable deprivation and suffering.

Those of us who undoubtedly want to do our Christian duty as individuals to other individuals but are disposed to regard as inappropriate any active concern on the Church's part for changes in the structures or orders of society need to reflect more seriously and with greater imagination upon the needs of the individuals we sincerely want to serve. To cite the same example again, who will calculate the amount of suffering the segregation system in race relations imposes daily upon individuals—constant injuries to self-respect, perpetual insecurity, the necessity of continually fighting one's way if one seeks to live like a normal person, the strange aloneness of finding oneself an alien in one's own land, the only land one knows? Who can measure the hurt of this for even one individual, not to speak of millions? I have myself seen an American Negro child, protected miraculously from his birth by his parents as many Negro children are, when he was first forced to recognize that in the majority opinion in his own city or town he was neither a citizen nor even a normal human being, but a thing apart. Can anyone concerned in Christ's name for 'individuals' forget a thing like this or be unconcerned about the social cause of it?

In a word, 'the Church's being the Church' involves a sensitivity on the part of its members to the needs of our brethren (whatever their race, nation, or class) in their full range; and it means whatever action in the political and economic sphere their needs may require of us. And, as I have said, this action will be demanded of us, not by any external authority or on the basis of merely secular considerations, but in virtue of our being as Christians; and by the same token the action will be characteristically Christian in motivation, 'spirit', and tone—an expression of the inner existence of the community of Christ.

*   *   *

This same existence sets up norms for the ordering of our personal lives under every aspect—norms of a distinctive kind because the existence is distinctive. There *is* a 'law of Christ', and it will not be identical with, and need not be even consistent with, any other morality, conventional or unconventional, which rests on other grounds. Often nowadays I hear, or read, arguments on issues of private or public morality, arguments in which Christians are participating but which proceed entirely on the basis of inferences from sociological and psychological data, and of generally accepted ethical principles, without any reference at all to the Church's distinctive existence and to the ethical implications of that existence—the considerations which, one might suppose, would be for the Christian the decisively important ones. Listening to such arguments and the conclusions they sometimes come to, I remember a sentence of the author to the Ephesians—appearing, significantly enough, in connection with a reference to sexual morality—and find in it a fresh meaning and relevance: 'Ye have not so learned Christ.' Is not this the criterion the Christian will apply to his beliefs about what conduct is required of him, or is permitted to him, in every situation—indeed, in many kinds or classes of situations (although I am not meaning to enter into controversy about 'situation ethics')? And will he not find many ethical conclusions, however plausible on other grounds they may be, in the end impossible for him simply because they are incompatible with what he knows and shares in as a member of the Church?

I am not for a moment suggesting that we shall always thus find simple and sure answers to our ethical problems or that we are thus dispensed from seeking all possible light from every available source upon all of them. My only point is that there are implicit ethical commands in Christian existence and that the Christian's decision in every ethical dilemma will, if authentic, involve a listening to, and a primary loyalty to, these commands. 'This,' he will find himself often saying, 'I cannot do: I have not so learned Christ'; or, 'This I *must* do; I have learned him so.'

*   *   *

This text from Ephesians might have served as the text, not of this chapter only, but of this whole book. For by 'learning

Christ' is not meant simply remembering the reported teaching and example of Jesus and accepting their truth and authority. 'Learning Christ' is listening to the Spirit of Christ in the living Church and being guided by what one hears. And is not the question of how we have 'learned Christ', in this sense of the phrase, the test of rightness and truth with reference to all the themes we have considered, and any other possible ones? Is a certain belief, theological or ethical, necessarily implicit in, necessarily presupposed by, the reality of Christ— that is, by the inner reality of the Church, the community of the Spirit? Then, we have been saying, it must be deemed true and essential. Or can it be said about this same belief that, although it is not in conflict, or inconsistent, with the reality of the Christian existence, it is not thus *required* by it? Then, we would need to say, the belief may be judged true or false, but, in any case, it cannot be regarded as essential. If, however, the belief represents an inescapable denial of what is necessarily implied in that existence—when one is forced to say about it, 'We have not so learned Christ'—then, there is no alternative to one's rejecting it as false and divisive. We—even 'we . . . who have [been given] the first fruits of the Spirit'—may well differ as to how a particular belief is to be classified. But if we agree as to the *basis* of judgment—namely, that true and essential beliefs will answer to, and be required by, what is real and essential in the life of the Church—can our differences be very wide or very important?

*   *   *

Greater unanimity, as well as greater firmness and clarity, in our believing waits for a revitalization of the Church itself. For all its apparent weakness ('not many wise . . . , not many mighty, not many noble'), Christianity began magnificently, stepping from the soil of Palestine on its westward march with the tread of a conqueror. It feared neither the power of men nor the wisdom of men. It dealt with Caesar and honoured him, but it did not bow to him. It spoke to philosophy and listened to her, but it did not sit at her feet. It had a power of its own and a wisdom of its own—and was fully aware of having both! One is not being wistful or nostalgic in recalling this. So must it be again! So shall it be again!

Some three or four decades ago, Will Durant wrote prophetically: 'We move into an age of spiritual exhaustion and despondency like that which hungered for the birth of Christ.'[1] Could any prediction more surely have been fulfilled? Do we not, every one of us, feel to some degree the awful weight of the impossible burden modern man, for all his amazing achievements, has chosen, in his blindness and pride, to take on his own shoulders? And can the hunger of our age be described except in some such words as Durant used? Christ must be born again—that is, the Church must recover its own inner truth and integrity as his body, must realize afresh its own nature as a communal sharing in the love of God made known to us in him and including all men in its embrace. We shall know again what we *believe* when we know again what we *are*.

The renewing of the Church's true life we can never ourselves contrive or bring to pass; life is always God's gift. But only if we know so poignantly our need of it—our utter futility and emptiness without it—that we shall desire it with our whole heart and set it above our pride and every earthly thing—only then can we wait for it with hope. For we can have it if we want it. 'Ask and you shall receive; seek and you shall find; knock and it shall be opened to you' may not apply to our wants for many lesser things; but it is the very truth of life if what we want is this thing. 'Maranatha, Come, our Lord'—

On the Meaning of Life (London: Williams and Norgate, 1933).

this, Paul tells us in effect, was a prayer of the primitive Christians; and across the centuries we can sense the conviction, the yearning, the hope in that cry. When we reach the point of being able really to pray that prayer again, of really loving his appearing, there is no doubt that he will appear, not necessarily on the clouds of heaven, but still in his unmistakable identity, in all his glorious beauty, and with all his healing power. He will make whole both his Church and our hearts.

> Come, thou long expected Jesus,
> Born to set thy people free.
> From our fears and sins release us;
> Let us find our rest in Thee.

INDEX

INDEX

Alexander the Great, 60, 61
Anglican churches, 21
Anselm, 17
Apostles' creed, 16
Arianism, 26
'atonement', 64
Augustine, 17, 31, 84-5, 90

belief,
    Christian, 16-17, 20, 22
    of Christian about Church and
      Christ, 67-8
    Church's basic, 68
    and criterion of consistency of
      truth, 51
    experience and, 78
    intellectual b. and the Christian,
      14-15, 18, 44
    limits of Christian, 22-4
    and orthodoxy and heresy, 25-6
    and prayer, 20-2
    question of essentiality, 12, 14,
      17
    status in life of Church, 28
    worship and, 21-2
beliefs,
    Church's indispensable, 100
    criteria of essential, 45-7
    of early Christians, 24
    essential Christian, 41, 45-7, 51-2,
      53, 61, 76, 117
    essential about Jesus, 61, 70-1, 74-6

about God and Christ, 81-3
    necessity for adequacy, 47, 52
    'principle of economy', 45-7, 48,
      51, 52
    true b. and reality, 48-9, 51
Berkeley, George, 17
body of Christ, 103, 113, 118
Bradford, Gamaliel, 84
Brandon, S.G.F., 74n, 75n
Bultmann, Rudolf, 72, 72n, 73

Casserley, J.V.L., 25, 26
Christ,
    God's action in, 25
    hope in, 103-4
    significance of term, 82
    'uniting of all things in', 97
    See also Church, Jesus
'Christian atheism', 93
Christian ethic, 29, 108-9, 115-16
    social character of, 109-11
Christianity,
    a cultural reality, 73
    diversity of early, 23
    essentially an existence, 17, 19-20,
      33
    language of, 17
    not an ideology, 15, 33
    power of primitive, 117-18
    primitive and hope, 98
    relations with Judaism, 69-70
Christology, 67

Church,
  and belief, 24-5
  and belief in actuality of Jesus, 70,
    71, 73
  a 'colony', 98, 109
  and communication between God
    and man, 55
  as community, 12, 13, 34-8, 61,
    62, 66, 108-9, 114, 117, 118
  corporate social reality, 110
  and crisis of belief, 11-12
  and critical research, 62-3
  and criticism of social order, 111
  existential reality of, 12-13, 14,
    17, 20, 28-9, 30, 34, 37-40, 53,
    56, 57, 62, 68, 108
  'felt relationship' with Jesus, 39-
    40, 70
  form of, 37
  and heaven, 106
  and historical research in Jesus'
    life, 71, 73-4
  hope characteristic of early, 97-8,
    100
  implications of existence, 79
  kinship with Israel, 39-40, 68-9,
    70
  language of, 15-16, 29
  and memory of Jesus, 40, 70,
    71-2, 74, 92
  mission of, 109
  and new orthodoxy, 26-7
  normative value of early, 23
  participation in existence of, 30-1,
    34, 55, 108
  and 'picture of Jesus as the Christ',
    72-3, 74
  and racial conflict, 112-15
  relevance in present age, 13

  renewal and revitalization, 13,
    117, 118
  self-revelation of God in, 40, 54,
    57, 62
  and social action, 111
'common faith', 23-4
cosmos, 31, 48, 82, 89, 94
creation, 94
creeds, 16, 17, 20, 24, 28, 77, 99
criticism, need for, 45-7, 49
Cullmann, Oscar, 75n

death,
  actuality, 103
  in God, 104-5
  of Jesus, 61
  transformation of self in, 105
Durant, Will, 118

Eastern Orthodox, 35
ecclesiology, 67
Eliot, George, 101
Ephesians, Epistle to, 36, 116
Episcopal Church, 21
  Report of Commission, 21-2, 25
'eschatological community', 97-8
eschatological expectation, 97
ethics, Christian, 29, 108-11, 115-16
event,
  of birth of Church, 40, 57-8, 61-2,
    63, 65, 67, 68
  of Christ, 69, 79
  and christological story of Jesus,
    76-7
  individual the centre and focus of,
    59-61
  inseparable from history, 58-9
  Jesus centre of, 58, 67, 76, 92
  meaning of term, 58-9

evil, 94, 104
existential knowledge, 33-4, 63
experience and belief, 78

faith,
    in God, 98-9
    meaning of, 56
    'moment of', 72-3
    objects of, 100
Farmer, William R., 74n, 75n
Fathers of the Church, 26, 36, 98
Fourth Gospel, 109
freedom of thought, 32-4

'glory', 102, 106-7
God,
    Beginning and Ground of exist-
        ence, 88, 89
    Christian meaning and experience,
        81-4, 89-90
    'the companion', 86, 87-9, 91
    as Creator, 88, 89, 94, 95
    as defined by philosophy, 82, 93,
        95
    denial of reality and transcend-
        ence, 93, 94-5
    distinctiveness of Christian ex-
        perience of reality, 90-3, 95-6
    End of existence, 88, 89
    'Father of our Lord Jesus Christ',
        54, 55, 69, 81, 90, 96, 101
    Fulfiller of existence, 88, 89, 94,
        95, 98
    full vision of, 101
    idea of, 16-17
    of Israel, 39, 68, 69
    knowledge through Christ, 83, 98
    love for, 105

    love of, 64, 95, 98-9, 101, 105,
        106, 107, 108
    loving purpose, 64, 98
    orthodoxy and variety of beliefs
        about, 25
    peace of, 88
    people of, 39-40
    personal character of relations
        with, 95
    and prayer, 21
    and priority of existence to belief,
        90
    reality of, 40, 48, 70, 81, 83, 84-5,
        87, 88-94
    saving action, 64, 65-6, 95
    self-revelation in Church, 40, 54,
        57, 62
    and 'special revelation', 91-2
    as Sustainer, 94, 95
    and three stages of religion, 86-9
    and torment of human living,
        85-6
    undiscoverable and inescapable,
        85-8
    universal meaning and experience,
        82-9, 92-3
    unsearchable, 96
gospel,
    evidence of, 80
    proclamation by Church, 54

heaven, 105-6
heresy, 23, 25-6, 52
history, relation to event, 59-60
hope,
    contemporary weakness, 100-1
    of life everlasting, 25, 97-8, 99-106

imagination, role of, 46

immortality, 101, 103-4
'In the end God', 105
Israel, 39-40, 68

James,William, 48
Jesus,
    actuality, 70-1, 73, 74, 77, 78, 83
    centre of Church's life, 79
    centre of event, 58, 67, 76, 92
    as Christ, 62, 72
    christological story, 76-7
    as Event and as Person, 69, 76, 79
    existence of, 73-4
    and existential communication, 55
    explanation of event of, 76-7
    and historical research, 71, 73-4,
        82-3
    as Lord, 40, 67, 70, 79, 91, 96
    as man, 68
    memory of, 40, 70, 71-2, 74, 74n,
        75n, 78, 79, 83, 91
    picture as the Christ, 72-3, 74
    preaching of, 110
    relation to history, 61
    resurrection, 61, 70, 75, 77-9, 102
    a Zealot?, 74n, 75n
John, 23, 31
Judaism, 69-70, 90, 97

kingdom of God, 110

language,
    Christian, 17
    of the Church, 15-16, 17-18, 24
    and expression of belief, 18-19, 28
'law of Christ', 115
Law,William, 80, 80n
'learning Christ', 116-17
Leibnitz, G.W., 17

lex orandi, lex credendi, 20-1
life,
    after death, 29, 100, 102
    hope of everlasting, 25, 97-8, 99-
        106
Lippmann,Walter, 100
liturgical reform, 21-2
living, torment of human, 85-6
logic, 33
love,
    fellowship in, 40
    God's, 17, 64, 95, 98, 101, 105, 107
    for God, 84, 101, 105
    in the world to come, 101

man, need for 'salvation' and 'atone-
        ment', 64
Maranatha, 118-19
Marcionism, 69
martyrs, 36
Marxism, 15
memory,
    God's, 101
    of Jesus, 40, 70, 71-2, 74, 74n, 75n,
        78, 79, 83, 91
Methodists, 35
miracles, 61, 78-9
Moffatt, James, 98
'moment of faith', 72-3
mythology and language of the
        Church, 16

Napoleon, 60, 61
Negroes and whites, 112, 115
Nestorianism, 26
New Israel, 69
New Man, 57, 76
New Testament,
    and Christian ethic, 110

and Church, 56-7
emphasis on hope, 98
and life beyond death, 102, 103-4
and 'objectivity' about Jesus, 55
writers, 36-7, 56
Nicene creed, 16, 99
nirvana, 103

obligation, Christian sense of, 40,
    108-9
Ogden, Schubert, 55
orthodoxy,
    criterion of, 21
    and heresy, 23, 25-6
    new, 27

Paul, 23, 31, 36, 75n, 98, 119
    conception of New Man, 57
    on 'faith, hope and love', 98-9
    on life of world to come, 102
    and meaning of faith, 56
    and reality of God, 92
Pentecostals, 36
Peter, First Epistle, 23, 36, 102
Pittenger,W. N., 87n
Plotinus, 17
prayer,
    and belief, 20-2
    of primitive Christians, 118-19
Prayer Book, 21, 22
preacher, 36
    and interpretation of life of
    Church, 31-2
prophets, 36, 69
Protestants, 36, 110, 112
psalms, 69

Quakers, 36

racial discrimination, 112-15
reality,
    knowledge of, 44, 47-9, 50
    openness to, 48, 51
    relationship with theology, 52
redemption, 80
reformers, 36
religion, God and three stages of,
    86-9
research,
    and the Church, 62-3
    into Jesus' life, 71, 73-4, 82-3
resurrection,
    of the body, 103
    of the dead, 99, 100
    of Jesus, 61, 70, 75, 77-9, 102
    of the self, 105
Revelation, Book of, 102
revelation, special, 91
Roman Catholics, 35, 110, 112
Russell, Bertrand, 84-5, 90

saints, 36
salvation, 64, 103
science, 19, 100
self,
    fulfilment, 105-6
    resurrection, 105
Sermon on the Mount, 75n
Simkhovitch, V. G., 75n
space, 106
Spinoza, Baruch, 17
Spirit, the,
    Church and awareness of, 65
    existential knowledge of, 78
    experience of, 40, 70, 108-9, 114
    full life of, 106
    and God's love, 40, 70, 99, 107,
    108-9

'joy', 'peace', and 'hope' in, 17
loss of sense of reality of, 101
new life of in body of Christ, 103
reduction to subjective phenomenon, 95
share in new life of, 101
symbolism of Church's language,
15-16
systematic theology, 54

technology, 100
theologian,
fivefold task of present-day, 28-9
and intellectual freedom, 32-3
necessity for participation in existence of Church, 30-2, 41
no 'pure', 42-4
theology,
Church first object, 53-4, 55
Church thinking and formulating,
54
Church's existence presupposition
of, 30, 41
close relationship with reality, 52
existential basis, 42-4
relation of 'natural' to 'Christian'
and 'revealed', 41-2, 44
systematic, 54
thinking, necessity for the Christian,
45

Thomas Aquinas, 17
Thompson, Francis, 84, 85
Tillich, Paul, 17, 71-2, 73
Tilson, Everett, 55, 55n, 56
time, 106
truth,
affirmation and denial of, 33
coercive power, 45
creed and, 28
expression of, 19, 29
'revealed' and experience, 44
theological, 22

Unitarians, 36
'uniting of all things in Christ', 40

virtues, three supernatural, 99-100

Wedel, Theodore O., 23, 23n
Whitehead, Alfred North, 17, 86-7,
87n, 90
Wieman, H. N., 87n
'will to believe', 48
William of Ockham, 17
world, reconciliation to God, 64
world to come, life of, 99, 100-1
worship of Church, 20-2, 54

Zealots, 74n, 75n